DISCONNECTED

DISCONNECTED

Parenting Teens
in a MySpace World

CHAP CLARK
AND DEE CLARK

BakerBooks
Grand Rapids, Michigan

Published by Baker Books
a division of Baker Publishing Group
P.O. Box 6287, Grand Rapids, MI 49516-6287
www.bakerpublishinggroup.com

Printed in the United States of America

Library of Congress Cataloging-in-Publication Data
Clark, Chap, 1954–
    Disconnected : parenting teens in a myspace world / Chap Clark and Dee Clark.
        p.   cm.
    Includes bibliographical references.
    ISBN 10: 0-8010-6628-X (pbk.)
    ISBN 978-0-8010-6628-3 (pbk.)
    1. Parenting—Religious apsects—Christianity. 2. Adolescence. I. Clark, Dee. II. Title.
    BV4529.C5183 2007
    248.8′45—dc22   2007008588

Contents

Acknowledgments

This book could not have been written without the words written into our lives by the people we love the most: our parents and our children.

We dedicate this book to our parents—John and Gale Clark and John and Jan Carlson—who have loved us, guided us, supported us, and put up with us throughout our lives. As we have learned more about ourselves and this wild adventure called parenting, we have grown to appreciate each one of you more and more. Your willingness to share yourselves, your homes, your resources, and mostly your encouragement, even when we were bent on our own path, has shaped who we are today. We thank you, and we dedicate this book to you and your legacy in our lives and work.

We also dedicate this book to our three children—Chap, Rob, and Katie. The incredible privilege of partnering with the Spirit in trying to carve out of a wild and often hostile world the kind of environment where you could become the men and woman that God has created you to be has been the ride of our lives. You have not only soared beyond our wildest dreams, but you have also been our tutors along our family's journey. We can now say with full confidence and indescribable joy that you are our friends and our partners in God's kingdom work. We dedicate this book to you, and honor you for how you have loved us, allowed us to speak into your lives, and remained deeply connected to us. Lastly, we want to acknowledge those who have worked to make Foothill Community Ministries, Inc., and our ParenTeen™ and HURT Seminars a reality. The dream to get thousands of parents and caring adults to look more carefully at how our ever-changing culture has affected our kids and changed what it means to be a parent and a friend to them today is bearing great and lasting fruit. We thank you all, but first our original couples group, who had the vision for our work and ministry—Ralph and Judy, Jeff and Nancy, Rusty and Meredith, Dave and Annie, and Jim and Angela. Also, to our friends on the ParenTeen™ and HURT seminar teams, and especially Lisa Fraze and Katie Parsons, who have been selfless and passionate in getting our message out there. We are so grateful that we get to serve with so many quality and dedicated people.

Introduction

"What is REAL?" asked the Rabbit one day, when they were lying side by side near the nursery fender, before Nana came to tidy the room. "Does it mean having things that buzz inside you and a stick-out handle?"
"Real isn't how you are made," said the Skin Horse. "It's a thing that happens to you. When a child loves you for a long, long time, not just to play with, but REALLY loves you, then you become Real."

Margery Williams, *The Velveteen Rabbit*

Like the story of the velveteen rabbit, this is a book about what it means to be real. It may not be real enough for you, but after a lifetime of Christian service and leadership, we imagine that it might be a bit too real for most. We have set out to write a book for parents who don't want or have the time or energy for anything other than reality. We believe that in today's busy, fragmented, nerve-wracked world, what truly matters is often lost beneath the pretense of how life *should* be. And for we who align ourselves with the Christian faith, another layer is added to this: we somehow think that we are supposed to be immune from the daily struggles and heartaches that "other people" experience. Most of us work hard to project a layer of strength and stability, yet just beneath the surface, when we allow ourselves to go there, we fight this nagging feeling that we are not quite what we present on the outside. In the new millennium it seems to be a universal fact of life that we all struggle with this dichotomy—we can rationalize and defend with the best of them. But who of us is not on the run, at least sometimes, somewhere deep inside of us, and occasionally to the point of despair?

Today there seems to be an ever-widening gulf between how we live on the outside and what is happening under the observable radar we present to others. Most of the books we read and the messages we receive reinforce this commitment to propping up what we portray to others. What we don't often think about, however, is the cost of living life ignoring the struggles and complexity we face every day. We all want to be whole and to be free to live from the inside out, yet we seem to have so few people and places where we can go to be real and honest. This even affects our relationship with the God who has proven his love for us every day of our lives. We are afraid to talk about and uncover the truth about our fears, our confusion, and our loneliness, even to ourselves.

This is especially true where we are at our most vulnerable—in our friendships, our marriages, and our families. At the dinner table, in the family room, at the ballpark, and on the way to church, we struggle to maintain the illusion that we can handle life on our own and that if we keep moving forward, we will be fine. But somewhere deep inside of us, we *know* better. We are all too keenly aware that we *need* others, and their perspectives and their support, to be healthy and whole in today's fragmented society. Sure, the stories of successful parents whose diligence and effort has produced perfect Christian kids abound, but, honestly, have you ever known any of these families "up close and personal"? In our experience, few, if any, families are able to escape at least some level of struggle and pain.

This book is an invitation to enter into your child's developmental journey with the goal of handing them off to the Father who loves them and to the community they are called to embrace. Our desire is to provide a perspective on and an awareness of what your child does and will face as he or she grows up in today's wild, disjointed world. In part 1 we will look at the changing world of childhood and adolescence so you can understand what your child will go through growing up. Then in part 2 we will look at what it means for you as parents to respond to your child in this changing culture.

From Our Family to Yours

This is a book written from our own journey and experience. We both have been working with families and young people for years, Dee as a licensed marriage and family therapist and Chap as an author, speaker, and professor of youth, family, and culture. Our training and experience do influence much of what we say. But this book is more than a recitation of formulas and "professional insights." It is written out of our experience raising three powerful and deep kids who have stretched and challenged us every step of the way. They have taught us (and we are still learning) what it means to be responsible for the developing lives and faith of three of God's precious and beloved creations. This book comes from two parents who early on grew weary of trying to measure up to what the "pros" told us about how a good parent should look, talk, and act. We are tired of burying our heads in the sand and hearing quick-fix answers to the very real challenges that face us as a family every day. We know better than most, not only from our vocations but from our own experiences, how much pain floats around out there.

This book flows from the conviction that we as parents need all the help we can get as we set out to make sense of life and seek to love and nurture our children. Here you will find our story, including our joys and our heartaches. It is a story we have lived and are living. In this book we invite you to engage in the same daunting but essential parenting response to the craziness of our culture—to come alongside your child and deal honestly with the reality of the pain that he or she will encounter throughout life. At times this will take some intense reflection and the ability to look in the mirror. This book is meant to be a resource for you as a parent, one that will spur you to action.

Most of all, this is a book for our kids, because they deserve our very best—our best thinking, our best insights, and our best efforts. Our primary calling as a parent from the day our children are conceived to the time they become our adult peers is to represent God as we care for those who are priceless to him. As John Calvin reminds us,

> If we are not our own, but the Lord's, it is clear to what purpose all our deeds must be directed. We are not our own, therefore neither our reason nor our will should guide us in our thoughts and actions. We are not our own, therefore we should not seek what is only expedient to the flesh. We are not our own, therefore let us forget ourselves and our own interests as far as possible.
>
> We are God's own; to him, therefore, let us live and die. We are God's own; therefore let his wisdom and will dominate all our actions. We are God's own; therefore let every part of our existence be directed towards him as our only legitimate goal.[1]

We have been parents for over twenty-five years. From the first moment we discovered that we were going to be parents, we have dreamed, prayed, wept, argued, and wrestled over how to be the best possible parents we could be. Our ultimate goal has been for our three kids to develop a firsthand, personal faith in the God who loves and calls them. The best chance we have for that is for us to do whatever we can to create the space and environment where our children get as clear a look at him as possible. Although some may think that the *spiritual* development of children and adolescents and their *psychological* and *social* development are different parental concerns, we are convinced that growing up is a single process and therefore, for parents, one package. In other words, we need to see the call to "train a child in the way he should go" (Prov. 22:6) not as being about only those things that most people think of as "spiritual" training but instead as being about the total call of life training. In this book, then, we want to help you to raise the complete child, with the goal of seeing the child form an authentic trust relationship with God and interdependence with God's people in community. As humble seekers who have joyfully ascended mountaintops and also crawled through slimy pits along the way, our intent is to write in such a way that you will be more encouraged and empowered than when you began the book.

Therefore, we pledge to do all we can *NOT* to:

- bore you. We will use illustrations and stories only when absolutely necessary to demonstrate a point, not to fill a manuscript or to inadvertently create the false impression that this is one more formula that "works" when you do what we say.
- insult you. There are two ditches to avoid when writing a parenting book: assuming too much and assuming too little. For some the sections on development may at first seem like recitations from a college Human Development 101 course. We have worked hard to avoid stale traditional assertions and at the same time unpack some of the more commonly accepted theories being worked on today. And some research in this book either has not been published or is very recent. Our goal is to help you, the reader, to know how to deal with our changing cultural environment and how it affects your child's growth and development.
- discourage you. Part of the reason we're writing this is to help people understand that the challenges facing parents have changed, and these data and observations can feel deeply disturbing and highly discouraging. One of the prerequisites of truth seeking is gathering as much information as possible in order to see clearly the road ahead we need to take.
- induce guilt. We have lost count of the number of sermons, talks, articles, and books that have left us feeling worse than before we arrived. Most of the time this result is subtle, and rarely if ever is it intentional, but a teaching style that points to the "shoulds" of life seems to have that effect on people more often than not. As we have spoken and counseled on parenting, we have come

to the point of being somewhat attuned to the triggers that spark disempowering guilt. We are also well aware of the widespread tendency to live our lives motivated more by guilt than by mercy, grace, and freedom. We vow to be as careful with this as possible, because we are all too aware of what a short-term and shallow motivator guilt can be.

Instead, we pledge to do all we can *to*:

- inform you. This is not primarily a "ten surefire tips to being a great parent" book. Instead, we will lay out for you the real life issues you and your child will face throughout the growing up years. We will offer some tangible, proactive steps, which, with the right attitude and commitment in place, cannot help but give you some tools to help you develop a supportive, nurturing, and loving parenting style. Based on the latest research on today's kids and families, our emphasis is on helping make you aware of what you will face and the most effective and proven ways to respond as a parent.
- prepare you. Obviously there is no prerequisite to becoming a parent. In every culture throughout history, parenting was simpler, as it was located within the values and traditions of the society, culturally passed on, and communally experienced. Not only did young parents have their own parents' help and advice, but everybody was committed to helping raise each others' kids. In most cases the roles and expectations of growing up were so fixed that being a parent was relatively straightforward. In comparison, we have all but completely dismantled a sense of corporate living, and that includes parenting. Maybe you have great parents who have done a good job of training you, and if so, that is a rare gift to cherish in today's world. But even for those who have the best models and mentors, life has changed so dramatically that all of us need as much help as we can get.

- encourage you. Beyond informing and preparing you, our goal is to help you to rise above the despair that many parents feel, sometimes just below the surface of day-to-day life. This book is written as an honest guide—informative, challenging, sobering—that still sees hope and wonder in what God can and does do with parents who are willing to adjust traditional expectations and culturally defined styles in order to become agents of God's mercy and grace. The Israelite army may have been paralyzed with fear as the giant Goliath taunted them, thinking, "He's so big, we can't win!" But as David may have remarked as he approached their nemesis, "He's so big, I can't miss!"

- motivate you. In contrast to guilting you into trying to be the best parent you can be (which doesn't work), this book is intended to help you make those small course corrections—in your attitude as well as your practice—so you can see that what you are doing is actually making a difference in the life of your child.

- free you. The central reason we have written this book and offer our ParenTeen seminars is this: We are convinced that God not only has equipped you to be the best possible parent for your child but also provides the power, skill, and insight you need to fulfill your role as he has created and called you. While parenting sometimes feels like an unnatural, difficult, and even burdensome task, our desire is to flip the script and see it as a grand opportunity for the broken and sincere believer to experience the power and faithfulness of God working in and through us. May this book enhance your sense of freedom in Jesus Christ.

As parents of three children—twenty-six- and twenty-two-year-old boys and our nineteen-year-old baby girl—we come as two parents who are on the road with you, sharing our story. We are just like you, a mom and dad who care deeply about our kids but much of the time feel as if we need a friend to walk with us through these days. We have sought to raise our kids to know and love Jesus Christ, to love others, and to have a healthy sense of self. We have worked hard to emphasize their uniqueness as created by God, and therefore we have tried to do whatever it takes to allow each of them to hear their Lord's voice above the noise of the world. We have raised our children to follow that call and to go wherever the Spirit of God would lead each of them.

As great as it sounds, it hasn't been an easy or pain-free road. We have had our share of struggles, of questions, and of failures. Whether it is how we have parented or what our kids have gone through, the road has been at times treacherous and bumpy and at other times breathtakingly magnificent and glorious. Along the way we held on to each other and the Lord and tried to truly listen to our kids. We have been committed to modeling for them an authentic faith of our own while working hard not to push them but rather to gently guide them into their own faith. We have learned a lot, done some things well, and blown it at times. Every step of the way we knew we needed help—first from Christ, but also from our parents, friends, church, and any other person who could help us. That's also why we've written this book—we want to let you know that you are not alone. Parenting is not for the fainthearted. Our children have been God's single greatest catalyst for growing us in humility of spirit and a deeper understanding of life and faith (and we'll share our family's story with you in the last chapter). We are on the journey with you.

Welcome to the adventure.

PART 1

Understanding Today's Adolescent Journey

"I *get* it . . . Now, what do we *do*?"

If there is one statement we hear more than any other, whether we are presenting a parents' seminar or counseling someone, it is this: "Tell me what to do." Everywhere we turn, from the media medical establishment to today's sermon titles, we have been taught that everything in life can be fixed if we only follow the seven easy steps to health, wealth, and happiness. So when parents have a sense of distance from their kids or a child seems to be spinning out of control, they go in search of that magic formula that will make everything all right. Oh, as parents, how we so often wish life were actually like that. Unfortunately, life is not. And when it comes to parenting in the midst of a rapidly changing and unpredictable society such as ours, not only do formulae rarely work, but they usually make things worse.

As we begin to unfold what it means to love and lead your child today, there is one axiom that we need to establish from the outset: your child is not a problem to be solved but a creative, talented, and unique gift to be understood, embraced, and ultimately set free.

This is not a "handbook" of the latest tips and techniques that will help ensure your child's success in a competitive world. We will not be able to tell you how to get your kid into the "best" college, make a varsity sport, or even become "nice." Because we live in a culture that evaluates who we are and what we offer by how we look (image) and what we accomplish (performance), we are going to take you on an altogether different journey in parenting. We are offering you, instead, insights into the soul and world of your child.

To do that, before we launch into specifics on how to respond to your child's needs and life as they go through adolescence, we need to prepare you for this season by painting a picture for you of who they are and what they experience along the way. A surgeon friend once told us, "The best prescription is obvious when we take the time to discover the clearest diagnosis." This is also true of parenting.

> Your child is not a problem to be solved, but a creative, talented, and unique gift to be understood, embraced, and ultimately set free.

Tips and tools are fine, but if they are delivered without understanding what is really going on inside and around our kids, we might actually be making things worse for them.

In part 1 we will bring you up to speed with the latest research on development and the adolescent world. The world you grew up in is long gone. Adolescence has tripled in years since you were a teenager—from roughly a five- to a fifteen-year process. As you approach this section, our goal is that you would be open, ask lots of questions (maybe even read this book with a group, or at least ask other parents what they are seeing and experiencing), and see if you might be drawn into a whole new awareness of how your child's life is different from your own. As you do, you'll be ready to humbly head into the waters of response, knowing who it is you are called by God to lead and lead in his name and for his glory.

1

Holding On for Dear Life
The Times, They Are A-Changin'

Come gather round people, wherever you roam, and admit that the waters around you have grown. . . . For the times, they are a-changin'.

Bob Dylan

Do you ever pause to marvel at how drastically life has changed since you were a kid? In our busyness and preoccupation with what is in front of us and just around the bend, this stark realization tends to sneak up on us at the most inopportune times. But when it hits, it can hit hard, to the point that we may find ourselves mourning the loss of a never-to-be-repeated experience. Perhaps it hits when we stop to look into the eyes of a tiny stranger in her mother's arms in the grocery store, or surfaces when we drive by a ball field and see kids actually playing without any uniforms or adult umpires, or is prompted by the incredulous look on our own kid's face when we try to explain how we somehow survived without a remote control when we were kids. Whatever it is that teases us into the subtle sadness of days gone by, it reminds us that the world we knew growing up has vanished.

Each year Beloit College in Wisconsin distributes "The Mindset List" to prepare faculty for the incoming students they will face. Here is a sample of their more recent reminders of the reality of the world for today's college students:

- Photographs have always been processed in an hour or less.
- They never saw Roseanne Roseanna Danna live on *Saturday Night Live*.
- They have always been comfortable with gay characters on television.
- Bert and Ernie are old enough to be their parents.
- An automatic is a weapon, not a transmission.
- Computers have always fit in their backpacks.
- Fox has always been a television network choice.
- This generation has never wanted to "be a Pepper too."
- Women have always had tattoos.
- Thongs no longer come in pairs and slide between the toes.[1]

Whenever we do stop and let ourselves think about how different life today is from when we were young, what strikes hardest is the accelerated rate of change that is occurring before our very eyes. Change is our kids' one constant in life. And often it is good and even necessary change. But the speed at which society is mutating can take our breath away. From the realization that the day you buy a computer it is obsolete, to trying to keep up with major league free agency, to remembering what night your favorite TV show is on, it takes lots of brain-RAM and energy just to stay current with the little things. Then there's the data that eats up much of our time and gets most of our attention, like the price of gas or how the stock market did today.

Funny, somehow this struggle to keep up with change hasn't managed to seep into our parenting worldview. When it comes to our role as parents,

> Change is our kids' one constant in life.

we can so easily find ourselves locked in a time warp. Like our nephew's cute little pit bull puppy grabbing a toy, most people sink their teeth into the certainty that teenage life hasn't changed much at all since they were kids. Each of us, including those who are well versed in and even coping well with rapid cultural and technological change, carries around inside of us such a raw, tender recollection of our teenage years that we have a hard time being objective about today. So we steadfastly maintain the aloof but firm conviction that somehow in the midst of this social sea of change, the process and environment our kids are growing up in is similar to our own experience.

Recall for a moment some of these memories: lunch, geometry class, hanging out with friends, homecoming week, cool coaches, walking to get to places, mean teachers, playing outside late on summer nights, "bad" kids, your best friend, PE uniforms (or "gym," depending on how old you are and where you lived), youth group. Sure, these wrappings still exist, and even if you were to casually peek into them, you might not notice much of a difference. But you would be way, way off. The shell is all that has remained over the years. Both the external systems pressing in and the internal mechanisms keeping the machine going are vastly different today from even fifteen years ago. Although in the albums of our own historical narratives time stands still, those days we knew, loved, and sometimes hated are long, long gone. And for the sake of our children, we must allow this truth to sink in. In order to provide the kind of proactive and intentional care they so desperately crave, they need us to understand *their* world.

Do You Get It?

This spring I (Chap) was invited to preach and present a ParenTeen seminar for a large, primarily Asian church. As part of the worship service, a thirteen-year-old middle school girl memorized and delivered to the congregation a poem she had written about her life. We were all mesmerized by this young woman, not only because of the honesty, clarity, and directness of her poem but also because of the way she delivered her poignant message. For someone to bluntly state how they feel to a huge gathering of their elders is highly unusual—especially a middle school kid, and most especially a *girl*!

Here's her poem:

> I've got some time to kill
>   until I'm not a teen, but being my age is harder than it
>   seems,
> adults always saying,
>   "oh you kids have it so easy."
> Oh please, you have no idea,
>   you make it sound so cheesy,
> all the social pressure, yeah,
>   we make it look like a breeze
> to steer through the popularity ranks.
>   But do you seriously believe
> that the peer pressure is bearable?
>   Oh, less than you may think,
>   sex, drugs, and alcohol,
>   the fight's a ship that's just about to sink.
>   Even being a Christian,
>   can be so hard nowadays.
> They say things like, "oh it's not cool"
> and its not just some cheap phrase.
>   You say we don't have to work for food and the neces-
>   sities of life,
> but we have to deal with people,
> and emotions can hurt like a knife.
> I don't think you understand,
> actually, scratch that, I know,
> because if you could get it,
> your respect for us would grow.
>   It's so hard dealing with all the pressure,
>   doing what's right is so much harder than it seems,

you have to polish your reputation, clean it up until it
  gleams,
but underneath,
  there's so many dirty lies,
  that cover up the ugliness that this generation hides,
just beneath the surface,
  is all sins of all our peers,
and sometimes it's hard to realize, that God can fix all of
  this.

Jessica, age 13

Jessica said it well—"I don't think you understand, actually,
scratch that, I know." Then she paused and stared at the crowd
of thousands of her elders.

Jessica's confidence hung over the adults in the congregation
like a dense fog. In that moment they were forced to face the
absurdity of their flippant assumptions. Before them stood one
of their children, looking them square in the eye on a huge video
screen, pleading with them to stop, to look, to understand. Her
audience just sat there, stunned. They were shaken and humbled
by their ignorance and prejudgment, put in their place by a
beautiful, not quite child but clearly not adult member of their
community. Perhaps as the hours and days wore on, many could
forget the impression of that moment, but we pray that most are
haunted by Jessica's poem. We know we are, and we have given
our lives to caring for kids.

Do you ever hear yourself saying things like, "when *I* was in
high school . . ." or, "the way *my* parents disciplined *me* . . ." or
worse yet, "I know what you're going through because I've been
there"?

These are just a sampling of the kind of indicators that may
signal that in fact we don't get it when it comes to understanding today's world for kids. We have seen countless adults who
are convinced they are hip and savvy when it comes to their
children, when in fact their ignorance and blindness run deep.
In other areas of life, they regularly if reluctantly recognize how
time's march and culture's push have changed everything around

us. But something happens to us when it comes to our ability to objectively enter into our son's or daughter's experience of growing up. Our own memories are so vivid and fresh that we carry them around like a favorite picture, encasing them in a shrine-like memorial of those most sacred years of our lives.

Not convinced? If we were sitting with you right now and you were feeling safe and free, allowing your guard to drop for just a moment, perhaps you could see what we mean more clearly. If we were to play you a clip from a film or TV show, or maybe just a few notes from a dusty old album, immediately you would be transported back to your sophomore year of high school. It happens to all of us—why do you think the oldies stations have such a huge following? Do we really believe that Bruce Springsteen or Supertramp were that much better than Sean Paul or Rihanna? (Well, okay, but you get the point.) If you were to simply get a whiff of a fragrance like, say, Brut, we could send you straight back to that seventh-grade dance! (Even the people at Play-Doh get this, as they have recently introduced a bottle of perfume called "Eau de Play-Doh.") For every one of us, adolescence was such a volatile mix of pain and passion, sorrow and joy, anticipation and disappointment, that we all carry that cauldron of experience over our heart like a pendant. These memories cause us to fix our experiences in stone, over time cleaning them up and memorializing them forever.

Unfortunately, to be the kind of parent your kid needs, you have to somehow first recognize and then deal with how fresh your own experience is in order to rise above it. God's call to you as his personally chosen representative in leading and loving your child is to come alongside them with an open mind and a teachable, humble spirit. To be sure, your failures, fears, and heartaches as well as your past loves, accomplishments, and accolades are important elements of your own story, and even the painful events remain somehow precious. But as far as being a parent goes, your kid needs you to realize that those days are long gone and you have before you a child who is growing up and in the process of writing their own story. They need all the support and understanding you can give them. Memories are important to share, but only in their proper context and setting, not as a way to somehow show your child you "get it."

Simply put, the first step in being a parent in today's upside-down, anything-goes world is to make sure your kid knows that you care enough about them to work hard to "get it." They have grown up believing that nearly every adult has their own agenda when it comes to them, from teachers to coaches to parents. This feeling is reinforced every time they need to be understood but don't know how to express it, or they want to be hugged when they act like they don't care, or they long to be respected as an emerging adult instead of feeling ignored. Frustrating, isn't it? Yep, it is . . . and seeing that is the first step on the long road of being a great parent. You will never nail it, but you can work at it, and that will go a long, long way in convincing your kid that you are serious when it comes to being their biggest fan.

It's Got to Be *Real*

One of the amazing things about today's kids is that they can easily distinguish between adults who are sincerely interested in them and those who want something from them or who simply go through the motions. If you work hard at trying to understand them and their world as a result of your deep love for them (with no other agenda!), they will, in time, respond by letting you in. Your goal must be to constantly study your child and his or her world. Your role is to care enough to actively pursue them with mercy and affection and to demonstrate that you really want to get to know them better so that you will be able to encourage them in ways they can receive and trust. Love isn't encouraging them to be like you or like some other ideal you have in your head. Being the best parent you can be means empowering, encouraging, comforting, and cheering your kid on to be the unique person he or she was created to be.

Does that mean that we shelve the values and beliefs we hold dear while raising our children? Not at all. What it means is that we do our very best to first be aware of our personal agendas and then put them on the back burner. Just because I didn't make it into the college I felt destined to attend, for example, doesn't mean that I am justified in putting the burden on my kid to fulfill that dream for me. You may have been good at Spanish, but if your teenager is really good at and enjoys math, your role is to do everything in your power to give her the opportunity to excel and fully develop that gift.

That is what it means to be a parent, especially in today's world where, with few exceptions, you are the only one who cares enough about the big picture. A coach, teacher, or even youth pastor may be a great support to your child at various points along the way, but you are one who is there day after day, year after year, to encourage, develop, and deepen your child in the name and Spirit of Christ. So our job as parents is to continually work on knowing our kids and looking to help them as they grow, all in an effort to be there for them on their quest to discover who they are and where they fit. And as you've probably already recognized, the biggest challenges are to put the past in the past and to acknowledge and then let go of our own ultimately self-serving agendas, being the adult and taking the lead in creating the best possible environment for our kids' sake.

2

The Power of Love

*Before you were conceived, I wanted you. Before you were born, I
loved you. Before you were a minute old, I would have died for you.
This is the miracle of life.*

Maureen Hawkins

When I (Dee) was pregnant with our first child, we were, obviously, crazy with anticipation. Like most first-time parents, we could not help but fixate on the process from the day we found out we were having a baby.

Even our devotional lives were rearranged. Up until that point our prayers were focused on seemingly more "lofty" matters—ministry and relationships and romance. Now we were on our knees with concern over "ordinary" things, like health, safety, and money. Our every thought was focused on this new life being formed, or as Psalm 139:15 describes it, being "woven together" in the depths of my womb. What a wondrous, glorious time that was! We found ourselves mesmerized by the mystery and wonder of David's song from Psalm 139:13–17:

For you created my inmost being;
>   you knit me together in my mother's womb.
I praise you because I am fearfully and wonderfully
>   made;
>   your works are wonderful,
>   I know that full well.
My frame was not hidden from you
>   when I was made in the secret place.
When I was woven together in the depths of the earth,
your eyes saw my unformed body.
>   All the days ordained for me
>   were written in your book
>   before one of them came to be.
How precious concerning me are your thoughts, O God!
>   How vast is the sum of them!

Most every parent we've met has gone through a similar epiphany when they had a child. Like Dorothy opening her bedroom door after landing in Oz, a burst of fresh, vibrant color explodes around a couple when a child enters their life. We've had three children, and each birth brought a genuine and absolutely unique eruption of joy and humbling gratitude. Babies do that to us, even if they are not our own. It is amazing how new life touches us—you can see it in how complete strangers respond to newborns. Even if you did not actually carry your child, as a new parent you know what it is to be shaken to the core with emotion and wonder. It is one of the most glorious things about being a parent, and the experience is literally miraculous.

How often do you look back on that season? Are you able to go to those tender moments easily? For me (Chap), as a dad, the song "Butterfly Kisses" and the movie *Father of the Bride* still knock me flat. When I watch that scene where the dad (Steve Martin) sees his daughter float down the family staircase through a sequential collage of ages, I can't help but remember those years with Katie, our daughter. He first sees her as a little tomboy, then a preteen with braces, then a high school beauty, and finally as his adult daughter about to be married. Images like these stir us in places we barely knew existed.

What went through your mind and heart as you prepared for and experienced the birth of your child? Can you recall how you felt, what you prayed for, and what you talked about? Do you remember the night before that birth and what you did? Can you still tap into the raw emotion of holding your child for the first time and that initial grasp of your pinkie? Memories like these are a gift, for they have the ability, when we allow ourselves to be swept up in them, to recall what matters most. They also have the ability to ground us during the darkest nights, if we let them.

It is not just the fondness of the memories that gives us power to draw on as parents through all the seasons of life; it is also the beauty, naïveté, and innocence of the dreams we had for our child. Who among us hasn't watched our five-year-old at play and wondered aloud what career they would choose? What parent hasn't spent countless hours encouraging and affirming the unique gifting and limitless potential of their child? When our kids are young and we ponder what life will be like for them, imagine what (or who) they will look like, or wonder who they will marry, we are lifted above the blinders of the ordinary and can feel what it means to hope. But as they get older and more firmly assert their growing independence, much of the time we find ourselves nervous and can easily become critical. We tend to be harder on them and increasingly consumed with how they act, talk, look, and perform. The process grinds on until eventually our dreams for them are but whispers of a forgotten past. Eventually we find ourselves at the point where we are less concerned with the overall process than we are with how they look or act *today*.

So, parents, as you prepare to engage in the real-life issues you and your child face and will be facing, it is time to sit back, close your eyes, and take a deep breath. Grab some trusted friends to walk with you, and force yourself to pull yourself out of the tyranny of the ordinary and to recapture the hope and the dreams you have tucked away on a shelf in your mind. Like stumbling upon old videos while cleaning out the closet, you need to slow your life down enough to replay those memories so that you can step into what life was like when your child called you their hero. If you are still in this stage, enjoy it while you have it and cherish the time, knowing that the day will come when you will fall off that proverbial horse and become to them an obstacle in the way of their emerging freedom and autonomy. Although we as parents are just as tossed around by the winds and waves of performance and image as our kids, they are relying on us to be an anchor for them. As much as anything, they need safety and stability. Our job, then, is to be strong, to rise above the fray of life, and to fix our eyes on the goal of parenting.

The Goal of Parenting

During the final weeks leading up to the cross, Jesus was walking with some friends on what was likely a busy, well-traveled road. Somehow someone recognized him, and so began a near frenzy of adults shoving their children toward Jesus so that he could touch them, believing that just by his touch they would receive great blessing (see Mark 10).

For some reason we do not know, the disciples were greatly put off by this chaotic scene, and so they did what disciples are prone to do when their teacher has gotten himself surrounded by fans: they took charge and told the crowd to back off. When Jesus saw them "rebuking" the crowd, he turned on his disciples with indignation and said, "Let the little children come to me, and do not hinder them, for the kingdom of God belongs to such as these. I tell you the truth, anyone who will not receive the kingdom of God like a little child will never enter it" (Mark 10:14–15).

In this passage Jesus was more than bothered; he was deeply grieved. His reaction to the disciples' need to control the situation at the expense of the children prompted one of his most pointed, albeit brief, speeches: "Do *not* hinder them" (v. 14). The word translated "hinder" means more than to stop doing something; it also implies doing anything, even subtly, that would have the effect of keeping a child from Jesus. His statement "Let the little children come to me" (v. 14) in response to the supposed good intentions of his followers was made to make sure they knew *why* he was so frustrated. He had a deep and tender love for children, and his disciples didn't see it. Throughout the Gospels it is clear that God sees children as sacred and pure, and therefore he is adamant in his protection and nurture of them. Children matter to Jesus Christ, and anything that could hinder a child from getting close to him causes him great anguish.

Who would argue with Jesus in his clear preference for children? Children are not finished products. They are neither refined nor selfless. Children are marked by untamable energy, life, and passion. They are noisy, messy, wild, and unpredictable. They do not do well at staying in line for long or at remembering directions. Yet it was *children* that Jesus said *own* the kingdom of God! He didn't mind that they were unfinished products or that they had yet to produce any good fruits proving them "fit for the kingdom." Jesus's love for and acceptance of children came from a deeper place. They mattered to him not because of what they *did* but rather because of who they *were*.

So what does this have to do with the goal of parenting? Everything, for we as parents have been granted temporary custody of the kids we have been given. Just as he instructed his disciples that day to "Let the little children come to me, and do not hinder them" (v. 14), so too we have been given the ultimate task of making sure that our kids have the best and clearest chance to get close to Jesus, the one to whom they ultimately belong. We must do whatever it takes to get any hindrance out of the way of them encountering the true, alive, and real Jesus. That single calling summarizes your job as a parent. The point of parenting, after all is said and done, is making sure your child has had the best and clearest opportunity to get up close and personal with their Creator. Everything you say and think and plan and do for your son or daughter must be administered through this single filter. When you wipe away all of the layers, issues, and questions that we face as parents, in the long run the only question that matters is, "Is who I am, how I live, and how I parent providing my child the very best chance to see and experience the Jesus who died to redeem them?" Nothing will ever be more important for you

> When you wipe away all of the layers, issues, and questions that we face as parents, in the long run the only question that matters is, "Is who I am, how I live, and how I parent providing my child the very best chance to see and experience the Jesus who died to redeem them?" Nothing will ever be more important for you to consider as you love and lead your child.

to consider as you love and lead your child. Healthy development, a well-rounded childhood, and a safe and positive family setting are important for every child. As vital as these are, they are secondary to the higher goal of helping them to see and know and follow Jesus Christ.

As God's agents of this high calling, we have only one strategy, one tool, and one task: love. As the apostle Paul wrote to the followers of Christ in Galatia, "The only thing that counts is faith expressing itself through love" (Gal. 5:6). It is our defining task to remain dedicated to this single calling and sole strategy. Our kids need our commitment to helping them get close to Jesus, and to experience that, they need our love. It is love that compels us to honestly embrace the complexity of the process and culture of adolescence. It is love that provides for us the ability to break through our assumptions and our prejudices to recognize the gifted, capable, lovable person who hides behind the look of indifference or rebellion. And it is love that motivates and enables us to allow our children to be who they are as opposed to who we want them to be.

To put this into practice, however, is sometimes far easier said than done, especially today and especially in this culture. For many reasons bridging the gap between adults and kids is getting increasingly difficult, even for parents. As society has changed, kids have become more reluctant to engage the adults who are in charge of their lives. Trust is a major issue to them, and that is true for parents as well. Effectively reaching across the relational chasm, particularly when they hit the teen years, is more difficult than ever. We need all the help we can get to be strong in our focus and in our love.

Leading and Loving Our Kids in a Changing Culture

During the last few years we have been working with a team to try to understand adolescents' perspective on their lives and their world.[1] Our team is amazed at what we have found so far by observing adolescents close up for eight months on a high school campus and by talking to them in a variety of settings around North America. We asked them about some of the more central issues they face every day, like parents, home, sports, dreams, fears, friends, sex, school, alcohol, drugs, and the like. By no means have we fully comprehended the complexity of their lives or the way they see and experience the world, but we are getting closer. And what we have seen and continue to discover has left us almost breathless, with an even greater desire to know more. When it comes to how the bulk of adolescents view their families, we observed what Patricia Hersch, author of *A Tribe Apart*, saw:

> A clear picture of adolescents, of even our own children, eludes us—not because they are rebelling, or avoiding, or evading us. *It is because we aren't there.* Not just parents, but any adults. American society has left its children behind as the cost of progress in the workplace. This isn't about working parents, right or wrong, but an issue for society to set its priorities and to pay attention to its young in the same way it pays attention to its income.[2]

As we embark on this journey together, we need to acknowledge that based on our own upbringing and family history, we all have biases and assumptions that affect our parenting. When it comes to where kids are today and how we as parents should respond, we have preloaded tapes ready to play when any of a number of buttons are pushed. It is our responsibility, then, to work overtime to be consciously aware of these biases and assumptions so that we can thoughtfully determine what truly aligns with God's call to us as parents and what comes out of our own preprogramming. We can easily tell just by listening to ourselves when we have not put in the effort to become self-aware. A few dead giveaways might be things like this coming out of our mouths when we feel threatened or frustrated:

"Because I said so."
"That's how it is."
"Because I'm the adult."
"As long as you are under my roof . . ."

Each of these (and hundreds more) represents a parent asserting power in a way sure to shut off communication, relationship, and any possible power a child has developed up to this time. How can a child possibly respond when their mother says, "Because I said so," or a dad says, "As long as you are living under my roof"? As parents we need to get at what lies underneath such statements and make sure that we do all within our power to avoid letting our buttons get pushed to the point that we take it out on our kids.

It is an obvious fact that parents and children see life differently. Parents and children often assume that the way they view and experience the world is the *only* way to see and experience the world. This presents a series of relational challenges on its own, but even more important for the parent to consider is that regardless of how you see the life and world of your kid, the way your *child* sees all aspects of their life and world—relational, social, ethical—is what matters most as they grow up. *Your child's* perspective of their own world ultimately has the greatest influence over them as they grow up. Even when they come from great families and homes where parents work hard to try to understand their children, today's teenagers believe that life is hard, antagonistic, and dismissively impersonal. According to our research, by the time kids reach high school, they feel an almost overwhelming sense of isolation and loneliness. Even the brightest and best kids revealed to our team how damaged they feel under the pressure of what they see as constant evaluation and critique. This

> *Your child's perspective of their own world ultimately has the greatest influence over them as they grow up.*

feeling fosters a profound insecurity in nearly every adolescent, an inner disquiet that few can verbally pin down but all seem to experience. In order to parent well in today's image- and performance-driven society, where everything from body contour to SAT scores is scrutinized and criticized, it is vitally important to recognize that the inside of your adolescent child is a stew of conflicting thoughts and emotions.

That's what this book is about: trying to help you to understand your child to the point that you are able to come alongside of them and be, as Philip Yancey says, God's dispenser of his grace. Our hope is that you would become a deliberate and committed student of your child, and that begins with an openness and honesty that allows truth to surface. As parents, when we begin to look beyond the ordinary dialogue and daily rituals and ruts we so often find ourselves in and to peer deeply into our kids' souls, we are able to take the small steps necessary to get to the place where they trust us.

The "Separation" Myth

In order to be the kind of parent your child needs and longs for, there is one more thing that you must never forget, especially when the time comes when you don't see or feel it: *Your child wants and needs you to be involved in their lives and to love them.*

Within the pages of nearly every book on parenting lurks a cultural fable that we want to address at the outset. This myth claims that teenagers desire to "separate" from their parents and cling to their friends as they move out of childhood and begin the adolescent journey of preparing for eventual adulthood. The reality is simply far more complicated than this viewpoint allows for. Lots of people say that middle and high school students rely more heavily on and even trust their friends more than their parents. In some ways this is true for almost every kid. And yet, at the same time, in almost every case your child desperately wants to stay close to you. To some this seems like a contradiction, but it doesn't have to be.

The truth? Friends matter to adolescents, and the older they get, the more they matter. But at the same time, and on an even deeper level, they intuitively know how much they need their parents for support and guidance. Almost every kid feels this way. Simply put, both are true. Kids want to connect with their friends and, at least for a season, do trust (or *want* to trust) their friends more than their parents. At the same time, adolescents also adamantly want to know that they have a parent, and preferably more than one, in their corner at the end of every round. Friends are more fun, more like-minded, and less likely to criticize, but parents unconditionally *love* and are there for the long haul.

Underneath their words and behavior, kids are desperate for their parents—*both* parents—to care enough to stay close to them. What is perhaps even more surprising is that this is true even for those kids who send the exact opposite message—the "I don't need you or want you" message. But please be assured, your child innately longs for you to actively and intently care about them. The key is *how* we as parents show we care, how genuinely and on what basis our love is dispensed, and how consistently our message of love and engaged compassion is presented.

Don't give in to the separation myth. Don't let your kids convince you that you don't matter to them or that they don't care about you. Be confident that you matter to them far more than even they know. Continue to extend to your child genuine, consistent, honest, respectful love. Reclaim the passion, awe, and commitment you once couldn't stop talking about. Before you is your *child*, whom you love! Trust that love, and trust the process.

3

Love That Connects

There are two lasting bequests we can give our children.
One is roots. The other is wings.

Hodding Carter Jr.

Each day of our lives we make deposits in the memory banks
of our children.

Charles R. Swindoll, *The Strong Family*

One of the greatest and most often repeated parables of Jesus is what has been labeled "the parable of the lost son." In truth, this famous lesson from Luke's Gospel (15:11–32) is misnamed. It's really more about the father than the son. In a nutshell, this parable tells the story of a younger son requesting his share of his father's estate so that he can go off and live his own life in a foreign land. After living the high life and spending all his money, he resorts to becoming a day laborer for a pig farmer. In the midst of his poverty, loneliness, and starvation, he begins the long trek home, rehearsing the story he plans on telling his father.

Sometimes it's hard for us third-millennium types to get a 360-degree perspective on an ancient story. We can easily imagine a rebellious son making such a request. But in that culture and time, making such a request would've been like wishing your father dead. Adding insult to injury, the young son liquidates his portion, then travels to a foreign land (the land of the Gentiles), further distancing himself from his family and community. Not only does this kid lose his money to the Gentiles, but in an attempt to simply survive, he becomes a pig farmer—not exactly a chosen occupation for Jews, who lived by the laws of the Torah.

Most interesting in this story, however, is the father's behavior. He doesn't act like the typical Middle Eastern patriarch but rather acts like a father who loves his son so deeply that he's willing to be humiliated. He grants his son's request and gives him his portion of the estate. He then has to stand by as the son liquidates it—selling land that has been in the family for generations—in front of the whole community. And then he watches his son wander off to a foreign land, disregarding his family and home.

When the father sees the son returning from a distance, he picks up his long robe and runs out to greet him. The father isn't exploding with compassion for his son as a result of the son's rehearsed confession. His running toward his son, the embrace, and the kiss all point toward the father's unconditional and selfless caring for his son. The father's agenda was not about how others saw him; it was about his son. All that mattered to him was his son. Following the embrace, the father gives his best robe and his ring to his youngest son, signifying not just a welcome back to the family but a place of honor within the family.

How do we show we care for our kids? How do we let them know that we mean it when we tell them "I love you"? What does it mean for a parent to be compassionate?

When asked point blank, most adolescents say they believe that their parents "care" about them. But at the same time, they usually offer a qualifier: Most believe that their parents care from a distance. What adolescents mean by this is that although they know their parents are concerned about what happens to them, they sense an uneasiness to step in close. What they want, and *need*, is the kind of caring that goes beyond mere concern or interest—a caring that comes alongside, a caring that understands and empathizes, and a caring that is connected to them in the most profound sense of the word. How deeply our love penetrates hinges on four factors: whether what we do matches our words, how far we are willing to go with our love, how sincere and genuine our care is, and whether we are consistent.

Does How We Act Match Our Words?

Teenagers believe that while parents care, their caring is often expressed out of an agenda that is more about the adult than the child. Take school, for example. Kids know their parents care about what is going on at school, but they know that this usually translates into homework and grades and teacher reports. Hundreds of students revealed to us that their parents care more about scholastic performance than about how they are doing going through the multilayered and often inconsistent expectations of the educational system. To be fair, most parents care about both, but sometimes it is easy to become imbalanced in our approach to our kids. We know, or at least say we do, that we hound our children because we care and want what is best for them. Yet in the eyes of your child, this motive is so easily lost in the emphasis on outcome, and they believe that their performance is our chief concern. All too often they believe that the reason behind our focus on performance is that their weak academic showing may reflect poorly on us as parents or even cut into the dreams we have for them. This is true of just about everything in teenagers' lives, from sports to friends to activities to church involvement—they believe that parents have their own agendas and that their caring is connected to what they want and how it reflects on them, instead of truly caring about their children.

Last year at a high school football game, we witnessed an example of this firsthand. A player made an interception, and as

he was running off the field, fans erupting in enthusiastic support, several fathers in the stands started doing something we
noticed as odd. Rather than applauding like the rest of the crowd,
the men huddled around another man who was apparently the
player's father. They were congratulating *him*! They were high-
fiving the dad for what a great play his son had made. Maybe
this has been going on for years, but that night was the first time
we had noticed it. We were so taken aback that our next realization hit us only later—everyone else around them had joined in
on lavishing praise, including the surrounding mothers in the
stands. "Way to go, Dad, your son did well." Unfortunately, it
was short-lived. When this same player missed an extra point,
he yelled to his son, "What was *that*? Get with the program,
Son!" The other dads just shook their heads. This has become a
searing image of what happens regularly in the lives of our kids.
Without meaning to hurt, parents who find their pleasure and,
conversely, their pain in their child's performance—in sports,
school, looks, church, it doesn't much matter where—send a
clear message to the child: You are only as valuable as what you
do or, worse, how you make me feel about myself.

How Far Are We Willing to Go with Our Love?

What your child ultimately longs for is beyond mere caring;
your son or daughter wants you to show compassion.

Compassion is a powerful but often misunderstood word.
Today it has come to mean that we care about someone else's
life or circumstance, regardless of what we may do about it. But
originally compassion was used in a much deeper way, describing situations where our commitment and concern compel us
to actively get involved. Compassion in its essence means we
have no choice but to come alongside the one we care for and
then literally share in their suffering. This level of care goes way
beyond what most of us experience, but we know we ultimately
all long for this kind of care and concern. Growing up in a changing, unpredictable world that is fraught with hazards at every

turn, kids are desperate for authentic compassion. They do not want sympathy or, worse, pity. But every kid thirsts for a caring that is deeply interested and invested—not a caring that takes over and tries to fix but rather a compassion that is marked by the gentle and consistent quality of an authentic presence and identification with their struggles, a compassion that is unafraid to weep with them in pain or hold them in the midst of fear.

The prodigal's father broke with social convention and even the "common sense" drilled into him by his teachers and culture by running toward and embracing the son who had broken his heart. As Jesus tells it, the father "saw him and was filled with compassion for him" (Luke 15:20). The father's compassion for his son was not a "theological warmth" of religious obligation. In this story Jesus makes it clear that this scorned and spurned father, who had demonstrated such grace and dignity at his son's ridiculous and insulting request, did not write the kid off. He didn't sulk or pout. He didn't even chase his child. He watched. He waited. He stood on the road, peering ahead, on the tips of his toes, ready to spring the moment his son rounded the bend toward home. This is the compassion that love demands and Jesus makes so obvious.

What does this look like in real life, with our flesh and blood (at times) prodigals? Perhaps it is hard to put on paper, and unfortunately so few of us know what it feels like to be the recipient of such an embrace. The offer of compassion as expressed by a genuinely safe and tender presence is something every one of us is searching for. Can you remember the last time you were in need of a friend and at the right time someone came along, sat beside you, and listened to your story? Can you recall a time when someone entered your inner world without needing to advise you, or fix you, or try to explain away your ache? This is the heartbeat of compassion, and it is what all children need from their parents as they grow up. It is, in fact, the foundation of everything else young people need, for unless they are convinced that you care enough to walk with them as they move through this time of turbulent adolescence, they will find it difficult to trust you. At that point they will not let you into the sacred, vulnerable places of their lives where authentic relational exchange originates. Compassion is the key to unlock those deep places, and that is where they need you the most.

How Genuinely Do We Care?

Whenever we try to help parents grapple with the power their intentional and proactive love toward their children has, whether it is in a public seminar or in the counseling office, after a sigh of exasperation we often hear this comment: "Okay, fine, I get it. I am the parent, and therefore I need to *love* and *care*. . . . Now, what I *really* came here for was to find out how to make sure my kid becomes responsible, and respectful, and, you know, a good person! He is messing up and needs to shape up . . . *that's* why I'm here!"

Rarely is this sentiment offered with a rough edge. In the vast majority of cases, parents are deeply concerned that their kids lack some of the basic tools that are the foundation of society, like civility, respect, and responsibility. Good, solid parents can rip their hair out trying to find that elusive silver bullet that will do the trick and make their child into the compliant citizen they hope he eventually will become. In a world where values like respect, honesty, loyalty, and self-sacrifice are in awfully short supply, parents are justifiably concerned that their child may be among those who continue to perpetuate this trend. Add to this the hope that these character qualities will emerge from a sincere faith and that their child will become a devoted Christian, and the stakes for both parent and child continue to rise all the higher.

That said, what often happens in our quest to raise "good kids" is that we can easily slip into using our care and support of them as a bargaining chip. We are nice, fun, and kind when and *because* our child or adolescent behaves. When they are rude or insolent, selfish or arrogant, insincere or inconsistent, for many of us our first knee-jerk response is to display exasperation, disgust, or outright anger. We react in a way that shows how deeply our disappointment runs, and we end up losing our ability to offer the compassion they need to grow through their failures. This is a tough one for most parents, including us, because what adult wants to invest effort in self-analysis and reflection when we are convinced it is our kid that needs the correction?

Although that is the typical reaction of most parents when a child goes haywire, it is even more vital that we work hard at our own attitudes, behaviors, and strategies. Only as we are willing to look inside ourselves can we develop the necessary compassion that is the foundation of a meaningful and productive parent-child relationship. It's this deep-seated compassion that will help them to grow up in a way that sets free who they are. But on the other hand, as we have said, your child knows instantly when you have made the shift from their agenda to yours. They are so attuned to the subtext of your relationship—the message beneath the message—that if they smell for a second that their behavior, attitude, clothing, lifestyle, or any of a myriad of other things has caused you to slip into a mode of conditional care for them as a person, they will eventually slam the door on your relationship and the chasm between you will grow all the wider.

What is important to remember here is that while behavior, attitudes, and lifestyle are important issues that parents must address and deal with, these have to be separated from how we demonstrate compassion toward our children. Short-term failures and disappointments are simply not on the same scale of importance as the quality and depth of our relationship. Consider this: In order for your child to allow you to guide them through the murky waters of adolescence, they must believe you really and truly care—and not just when they please you and comply with your opinions but underneath it all, through every struggle, squabble, and fight. To maintain any kind of meaningful role in their lives, where your child grants you the permission to help them work through issues that may be difficult and (for them) countercultural, they must first be absolutely convinced that you, the constant herald of the need to grow up, are on their side. The essential thing to recognize is the need to make certain that your child knows that nothing they can do or say will cause you to lose your commitment of compassion for them.

Several years ago while house-sitting for some friends who were really going through it with their oldest daughter, I discovered this handwritten poem on the father's desk:

DAUGHTER 17 (author unknown)

I have a daughter 17
When she lies to me . . . I love her.
When she disappoints me . . . I love her.
When she doesn't live up to my expectations . . . I love her.
When she reflects poorly on my name . . . I love her.

"Now I can understand how when she pleases you . . . and
    obeys you . . . and fulfills you . . . ,"
you say.

But that's not what I'm talking about.
It's when she does none of these things . . . I love her
AND for a very simple reason:

I'm her father . . . and she's my child.

How Consistently Do We Share Compassion?

The third issue that affects an adolescent's ability to trust in and therefore enthusiastically welcome a parent's willingness to show compassion is our consistency. During several particularly tough months, it finally occurred to me (Chap) that I was not the dad I wanted and needed to be for our kids. With the gentle encouragement of Dee, my therapist wife, I slowly became aware that while most of the time I was a great father—a decent listener when I put my mind to it, a supportive friend, willing to go the extra mile for my kids—at other times I fell into patterns that communicated to each of our three children that I didn't care very much. As I slowly began to acknowledge this tendency of mine, mostly due to one relational disaster after another in a span of a few weeks, I finally had an epiphany that my inconsistency contributed to and at times even set the stage for my children's own behaviors in the family, like insolence and rebellion. What I had seen as their problem I was now able to start to view as mine. I was the adult, yet I had allowed my own temperament, convictions, and frankly, lack of discipline to create an environment of mixed messages and inconsistent communication. In my heart I believed I had been relatively consistent and my love for them was unquestioned, but in my behavior I had let myself be controlled by my own reactivity and need to "fix it *now!*"

I guess somewhere down deep I have long been aware that at times my misguided and self-serving sense of timing, to use but one example, pushed each of my three kids' buttons in a way that would eventually lead to a major brouhaha. It was, and frankly sometimes still is, at those times when I allowed myself to lose perspective, to not consider my words carefully, and to lose my cool that my kids have responded by losing their trust in the good times. As much as I wanted to make sure my kids knew more than anything else that I cared about them and their lives and their struggles and that I wanted to be there for them, when I would let my own tiredness, laziness, pride, control, or any other factor sneak in and encourage me to treat them without compassion, it affected our relationship. Perhaps this is why the apostle Paul warned us in Ephesians 6:4, "Fathers, do not exasperate your children."

Trust is like a child's savings account—it takes years to build up any kind of sizable sum, only to have it so easily blown away by one homecoming night misadventure! Because of our histories and emotional makeup, most of us sometimes tend to overreact to circumstances beyond our control. In our family's case the road to healing hasn't been easy, and in many ways our kids have been great tutors as we have worked together through those times and ways we have hurt each other. As parents we should and must maintain our ultimate authority while our kids are growing up. They deserve and need that. At the same time, any moral authority we have begins with our willingness and ability to do all we can to be consistent.

Ready to Go

Today more than ever, parenting begins with invested, authentic, and consistent compassion. Not the superficial compassion of our hectic world that flies over, runs on by, or stands aloof and above, looking down with disengaged but vocal empathy. Today's parent is called to offer the kind of compassion that says, "I love you and I care about you. And because I love and care, I want to know you, to hear you, and to stand with you as you grow up."

4

The History and Meaning of Growing Up

Making the decision to have a child—it's momentous. It is to decide forever to have your heart go walking outside your body.

Elizabeth Stone, *The Village Voice*[1]

Most people think that the period between childhood and adulthood, what we typically call "being a teenager," is a historical and universal fact of life. Urban myth simply assumes that the transition from the wonder, pliability, and innocence of childhood to taking on the mantle of adult responsibility has always been a process of experimentation, rebellion, and pushing away from society in general and parents in particular. The attitude expressed by the phrase "When *I* was your age . . ." represents this bias. "Kids are kids," one exasperated teacher told us, "and they've *always* acted this way!" And she isn't alone; lots of people—teachers, coaches, and parents—believe this.

In light of the changes that have taken place over the last few decades and even centuries, however, is it possible that this firmly entrenched assumption simply may not be accurate? Can it be that even as we so easily bemoan the sweeping changes we have all seen, we still keep saying that as culture "advances," our kids' development is not affected? Regardless of what society assumes or what cultural stories imply, those who study the issue of development hold a different opinion. On the historical scale, adolescence is new, different, and rapidly changing in ways that affect everybody.

Adolescence—How We Got Here

The most common way scholars describe the stage of life we call adolescence is as a *social invention of modernity*.[2] In every culture around the globe across time there have been two stages of life, childhood and adulthood. In the initial stages of communal life in each culture and society, the most precious resource of that community was their corporate story, or *metanarrative*.[3] At the same time, the most significant asset of the community was their children, for they were the ones to pass on their story and legacy, thus perpetuating what ultimately mattered most to the community. Children were led and nurtured with great care and deliberate attention, because adults knew that children were the key to the future of their story.

In the early stages of development of any given society, every adult knew that the welfare of each child was the responsibility of the entire community, not just their own parents. As noted in the title of Hillary Clinton's popular book, in the early stages of cultural development, societies recognized that it indeed "takes a village to raise a child." During these early stages children were trained, guided, nurtured, led, and eventually assimilated into and included in adult society. Occasionally this was marked by organized and formalized rites of passage and rituals, but more often the transition into adulthood was natural and organic. Either way, throughout history children were valued as important members of society and therefore carefully trained and led into adulthood. No child had to wonder who cared for them or who took responsibility to make sure they received all of the resources and empowerment they needed to grow into adulthood. They had no need to be concerned with acceptance, worth, image, or performance. Children were intrinsically valued and systematically welcomed *simply because they belonged to the community*.

So where did adolescence come from? Over time, in almost every culture, more pressing issues began to squeeze out this commitment and focus on children. As societies developed and matured, children sometimes became tools to be used rather than people to be developed or even became a nuisance to be pushed aside. As industrialization and colonialism became widespread, this was especially true in the Western world, where children more and more found themselves on the margins of society and treated as if they were in the way. As the middle class emerged and developed and nationalistic empires were being built, the dedicated nurture and guidance of children went from the central place in a community's long-term commitment to a sidebar on the societal periphery. This trend was subtle and took centuries to develop.

Although here we have greatly simplified the complex history of how children were viewed in Europe for several centuries, what we now see as a result is obvious. In past centuries children were invaluable assets, gifts of God (or "the gods") to be nurtured and assimilated. In recent history, children have increasingly been called upon to learn how to become adults without the support they need to accomplish the task. What began as a tiny snowball at the top of a large mountain, going largely unnoticed, began to pick up momentum. Just over a hundred years ago, those who observed family life and child development began to see a trend that had been going on for some time. No longer were we operating with two stages of the life span, child and adult; there now were three: child, adolescent, and adult. The emergence of adolescence was an invention by default, but we nonetheless created it. And this was a massive social shift, unprecedented in world history.

This brief synopsis is not intended to be exhaustive, as the factors that converged to cultivate the rise of adolescence are varied and complex. However, even this much history can help us as parents see how multiple issues coming together can affect how we live our lives today. Your child is part of a social chain of events that has been evolving exponentially for hundreds of years. What matters for you is that this began because adults had ripped away the nurture and guidance children needed to become adults.

As the years and centuries progressed in the West, society's commitment to the proactive and community-wide nurture and training of children slipped further and further into the background. Although adolescence as a physical and cognitive transitional period may have been in place for a very long time, what has changed is the isolation and independence of the stage. The adolescence we have experienced for the last several decades is a result of sweeping changes in cultural attitudes and systems. Society transferred the responsibility of nurturing, guiding, and ultimately assimilating the young from society itself to children. Kids are essentially on their own to become adults, and this is now true in nearly every modern culture around the world. Most contemporary societies, sadly, have learned well from us.

> Society transferred the responsibility of nurturing, guiding, and ultimately assimilating the young from society itself to children. Kids are essentially on their own to become adults, and this is now true in nearly every modern culture around the world.

At the turn of the twentieth century, what exactly adolescence was and what it meant was not at all clear. Books and articles were debating it, but in the early years some saw it as mirroring what was going on in biology (thus the name *adolescence*, at the time used most often in biological circles, from the Latin *adolescere*, meaning "to grow into"). Within a couple of decades scholars and researchers were beginning to give significant attention to this new stage of life. From the early twentieth century to the early 1950s, few laypeople thought much about this transitionary time of life. Through the Great Depression in the 1930s, through World War II in the early 1940s, and into the Korean War of the mid-1950s, circumstances forced most Americans to focus on survival, and the new stage of adolescence was limited to only a two- to three-year period anyway, so few people took notice. Those who did are today seen as social pioneers and heroes. They saw the needs of kids and responded with strategies and organizations—like Young Life, youth sports, and so on—that sought to care for kids and assist them as they learned what it meant to become an adult.

This began to change in the middle 1950s with the introduction of youth culture. Sure, before that some clothing and music and films basically catered to a younger crowd, but generally up to this time these were actually young adult styles and interests. It wasn't until the mid to late 1950s that musicians, filmmakers, and advertisers began to recognize the potential of this quickly growing demographic. Not only were the Boomers beginning to hit puberty, but adults were continuing to find ways to fulfill their own needs and desires, and adolescence was beginning to lengthen. Soon that demographic known as "teenagers" was a social force, and they started to flex their collective muscles, demanding lots of attention. By the middle of the 1960s, lines had been drawn declaring the animosity and separation between teens and adults (the "generation gap"), and the first few skirmishes of the culture wars began to be fought. Through the seventies and eighties we had developed such clear boundaries between the generations that it was obvious that we had embarked on a course of mistrust and generational fragmentation. And worst of all, there was no going back.

Although this vast and sweeping social movement more or less sneaked up on modern society, in only a few decades the reality of adolescence was solidified in our societal landscape. It had morphed into the phase of life where one has an adultlike capability for abstract thought, processing, and relationships but at the same time is essentially *on one's own* to figure out how to insert oneself into an individualistic and sometimes hostile adult society.

Over the past century we have come to affirm and believe that what we have described is simply how it is and that this is how life has always been and is supposed to be experienced. In our work and research we have not come across a single social scientist or theologian who has taken much notice of the dark side of this massive social shift. It is as if we as adults finally have given ourselves permission to abdicate our created responsibility to raise, nurture, guide, and assimilate our young—simply by giving them a label and a name ("adolescent") that affirmed that their isolation and aloneness was a natural and normal part of life. But the cost has been high, and we who have gone through it have lost a bit of ourselves in the process.

The good news? We have finally gotten to the point where lots of people are saying "Enough is enough!" and are ready to do something to turn back the years of neglect and abandonment we have collectively handed our kids. No one wants to be alone and consistently driven by unreasonable, often unreachable and unhealthy performance and image expectations. We all long for a time and place where we are received, welcomed, and embraced for simply being ourselves. We were designed to grow up in and contribute to a community that not only includes us but truly *wants* us. That's what this book is about—helping parents to quit trying to raise their kids the way culture has dictated and even the way they were raised and to instead tap into that inner place that knows God has a better plan in mind for his children.

The more we understand what adolescence is and what it means, the more we can take steps to address the lonely and often painful reality most kids call growing up.

Adolescence—What It Is

So what *is* "adolescence"? It can best be summed up in a single word: *individuation*. A word like this can sound a bit daunting, but the process itself is really rather straightforward. Individuation describes the path toward becoming a *unique individual*. Essentially, individuation is a fancy way of summarizing the overall task of moving out of childhood and preparing to engage in mainstream society as a peer with other adults. It is the process where we developmentally travel from a world where we do not have to think about who we are or what we do (childhood) toward a destination where we must have the confidence that we can not only survive but also thrive in the multiple relationships and expectations of adult society. It is where the various pieces that make up who we are and how we respond to life must come together as an integrated, whole person. Individuation has been used in different ways by lots of people, but in the case of your child growing up, it is what it means for him or her to become an adult.

As the overall quest of adolescence, individuation has several streams, or tasks, that develop the whole person. Beyond the common agreement that adolescence is the developmental stage of life between childhood and adulthood, no one standard describes the specifics of the process. In trying to nail down the precise tasks of adolescence, there are as many lists as there are developmental textbooks. However, most people who study development tend to agree that three main elements make up individuation: *identity*, *autonomy*, and *belonging*. It is not that each of these tasks represents a clean or rigid checklist that must be completed before someone can be fairly confident that they have moved out of adolescence and into adulthood. As we traverse adolescence, these are the three areas where we must achieve a level of maturity that is settled enough to enable us to function interdependently in adult society. A person, then, is said to have entered adulthood when they have relatively settled on who they are (*identity*), have accepted responsibility for themselves and their choices (*autonomy*), and are ready to find their way into adult life (*belonging*). Each of these represents a distinct passage, and yet at the same time all three interact together along the way.

Let's break each of them down.

Identity—"Who Am I?"

"Who am I?" is the one nagging question that to an adolescent is like a slow, annoying drip that never seems to quit. Getting up in the morning to face their day, sitting in class, walking the halls, eating lunch—every social situation forces an adolescent to live out of a sense of self that is desperately trying to settle. This is because adolescence is the place where we are faced with the dreadful prospect of having to act like we know who we are when much of the time we are not really sure if we have a clue. Parents will often say, "That's not like you," to which their kid, trying to avoid consciously having to deal with their inability to know what to say, may angrily reply, "You don't even know me! You *think* you know me, but only my friends know me!" Yet internally they are usually crying out, "Who am I? I have no idea!"

What happens as we move through adolescence is that we make the shift from not knowing or caring about who we are to eventually landing on an awareness of our own uniqueness as a person. This process is almost always a pretty tough road. A child, being dependent on their family, has no need to even consider the question of identity, for who they are is defined within and by the adults who care for them. Developmentally speaking, unless they have gone through an extremely traumatic childhood, they do not know anything different. As adults, by contrast, we tend to define ourselves according to our relationships ("I'm a wife and mother") or our role in society ("I am a neurosurgeon" or "I'm a youth pastor"). So while growing up a child is *dependent* on their family to help them know who they are and their place and role in society, and an adult is *interdependent* with others as they live with them in communal relationships.

But what is so difficult for an adolescent is that while they are trying to figure out who they are, they have to be *somebody*. So they face a double whammy—having to go through a complex identity discovery process *and* at the same time being forced by the many expectations they encounter to live like a settled, confident, put-together, unique person. How does an adolescent know who they are? By what criteria do they define themselves? That is the central task of identity for adolescents: *to discover the person they are as they attempt to insert and assimilate themselves into adult society.*

The quest for identity has been studied, debated, and argued for the last eighty or more years. Usually scholars talk in terms of "identity formation" as a way to describe what happens during adolescence.[4] This phrase represents a viewpoint that basically assumes that who we are is a product of the interplay between our genetic makeup ("nature") and our upbringing ("nurture"). Out of these two we end up being "formed" into the person we become. Obviously there is something to this, and the debate is far beyond the scope of this book. But when all is said and done, we believe that who we are is not something that is "formed" in the interaction between nature and nurture but rather is something far more intrinsically true about us—we are who we are because God has made us so.

> How does an adolescent know who they are? By what criteria do they define themselves? That is the central task of identity for adolescents: *to discover the person they are as they attempt to insert and assimilate themselves into adult society.*

One thing we can be sure of is that our identity is not something that eventually emerges out of our temperament or upbringing. The Scriptures make it clear that who we are is decided before we were even born. Our identity, ultimately, is not a consequence of the interaction between the genetic code we inherited from our parents and the family system we grew up in but is rather the result of God's decision to uniquely create us. Psalm 139 tells us that "my frame was not hidden from you [God] when I was made in the secret place. When I was woven together in the depths of the earth, your eyes saw my unformed body. All the days ordained for me were written in your book before one of them came to be" (vv. 15–16). God has *chosen* to create each one of us out of his sovereign will. Henri Nouwen, in *Life of the Beloved*, puts it this way:

> It is very hard for me to express well the depth of meaning the word "chosen" has for me, but I hope you are willing to listen to me from within. From all eternity, long before you were born and became a part of history, you existed in God's heart. Long

before your parents admired you, or your friends acknowledged your gifts, or your teachers, colleagues and employers encouraged you, you were already chosen. The eyes of love had seen you as precious, as of infinite beauty, as of eternal value.[5]

The fact is that each of us is uniquely and individually created by the hand of God himself, and who we are is precisely the person that God has created us to be. So the quest for our identity, and our child's identity, is located in our ability to get a complete picture of God's handiwork as he created it. Therefore our task as we help our kids answer the question "Who am I?" is to get all of the lies and half-truths and misconceptions out of the way so they are able to see as clearly as they can who God declares them to be. This is especially true in a world that defines them according to how they look and how well they perform. Your child is a unique masterpiece formed out of God's own mind and heart—his beloved child. The childhood and adolescent journey for them, then, is to get past any and all messages that would stand in the way of appropriating this truth in the depth of their souls. Our task as parents is to help them get to the point where they are convinced that they are and always will be defined by knowing and trusting that God knows who they are and that they belong to him.

Autonomy—"Do I and My Choices Matter?"

The development of autonomy, as distinct from identity, is more about being trained to handle and then learning to accept personal responsibility. This seems like it would be an easy thing for parents to help their kids through; what parent doesn't want their child to grow in the ability to act responsibly? As life has gotten more complicated, with less clear guidelines, markers, and norms to rely on, being able to decipher multiple and constantly shifting cues and options is not as obvious or simple as it may at first sound.

Take the moral issue of cheating in school, for example. Say a close friend of your kid needs help because of a late night talk with the youth pastor after church the night before. He asks your kid to let him copy the homework assignment so he doesn't have points taken off. Deciding between giving a friend a homework assignment on the way into class versus letting the friend fail causes three conflicting values to get into a major "scrap"—loyalty to a needy friend, doing "what is right," and the ever-present fear of getting caught cheating. In a situation like this, your child instinctively knows that each of these values needs to be measured, evaluated, and analyzed in making the "right" decision. In this case she has to wade through these conflicting values and streams of ethical choices and consequences and instantly make a decision. This is not an isolated situation. Every day an adolescent has several dozen (at least) similar choices to make, and they all factor into a developing sense of personal autonomy.

Some use the phrase *locus of control* to describe what it means to take responsibility for one's life and choices. Locus, meaning "center of activity," can refer to the source of someone's ability to make decisions as they move through life. It is usually described as being somewhere on a continuum between external and internal locus of control.[6] During childhood, for instance, the locus of control is primarily external, meaning that the parents are responsible for that child. As adults, the more developed our sense of personal power and ability and our willingness to take responsibility for our choices, the stronger our internal locus of control. An adolescent, then, is shifting from having an external to having an internal locus of control.

How do you know when you have landed far enough in the area of autonomy to be an adult? Say you have a job and your boss calls a meeting for 8:00 a.m. An adult shows up at 7:55, pen poised, Palm handheld ready to go. Someone who rushes in a little after 9:00, latte in hand, whose only explanation is "Dude! They need to hire more people!" probably still leans in the direction of an externalized locus of control ("It's not *my* fault!"). Certainly each of us has some residue left over from our own incomplete and even unresolved adolescent experience, and we all play the "blame game" to a certain extent. But like identity, the development of personal autonomy and an internalized locus of control, while not exact and easily measured, is an essential developmental process that we all must grow in to become an interdependent adult.

Belonging—"Where Do I Fit?"

You and I were designed and created to need others, yet we live in a world where our fundamental metanarrative shouts individualism. Following that famous Horatio Alger myth, we continue to encourage kids to "pull yourself up by your own bootstraps." We are told it is best not to need anyone and that we must be strong and independent. But we all intuitively recognize our desperate need to be connected to others and to be a part of a safe and authentic community. This is how we were designed, both men and women. God did not create us to go through life alone but rather has built into us the need to live together in intimate and mutually supportive relationships while we both personally and corporately depend on him as our Father.

As our children go through adolescence, this dichotomy presents a unique and at times extremely difficult dilemma for them. On the one hand, they must become independent to grow into the person they were created to be. In fact, in a world that no longer assumes responsibility for nurturing, training, and receiving our kids into society, they cannot enter the adult world as a peer until they have developed enough of an internal, independent strength to be able to function interdependently. However, while they are going through the process of individuation, they also know how alone they truly are. No one can walk this road for them—not parents, friends, or family. As we will see, loved ones and supportive friends can be a guide, a support, and a safety net, but ultimately the very nature of this new invention of society we have handed our kids demands they go it alone. Yet they feel and *know* they need to belong . . . *somewhere!*

The three tasks of adolescence—*identity*, *autonomy*, and *belonging*—are waging a battle within the soul of every adolescent. They want to be safe and be held, yet they know that they must continue on toward that elusive and undefined thing known as adulthood. We as a culture have given them little help and even less hope (which we'll talk about in the next chapter), yet we as an adult-controlled society still stand back and collectively criticize, critique, and evaluate "those rebellious and spoiled kids." This is the journey we have handed our kids, and while it is their lot, it is not their fault. They need all of the understanding and, yes, compassion that we can muster to help them along the way.

As a parent you are on the front lines to reverse this flippant and destructive neglect. You care, and that goes a long, long way for your child as they try to figure out who they are, how to be responsible, and where they fit.

5

The Changing Nature of Every Child's Journey into Adulthood

Don't limit a child to your own learning,
for he was born in another time.

Rabbinical saying

When my kids become wild and unruly, I use a nice, safe playpen.
When they're finished, I climb out.

Erma Bombeck

We've all seen the contrast. On one side of the street are young mothers watching over their precocious, energetic toddlers, who are running wildly in a gleeful ritual of celebration. On the other side is a group of fifteen-year-olds sullenly staring into space, wearing their boredom and hardness like a badge. To those who would just take the time to notice the contradiction, it is startling. What happens in a few short years that robs the delight from a child and replaces it with the detachment of adolescence?

Where did that kid go?

That is where we must go now—into the heart of the adolescent experience—trying to understand not only how it is different from when we were growing up but also how kids have responded to the world we've handed them. In chapter 1 we talked about change. Not only has adolescent culture changed, but the impact of the *rate* of change in almost every aspect of contemporary life is catching all of us off guard. This is true for the nature of development as well, for both children and adolescents.[1] What was a more or less stable progression during the middle part of the last century has morphed into a lengthy, volatile, and highly complex process. Being willing to come alongside your child, becoming a careful student of their life and world, and appreciating them for the evolving complexity of the journey is where we go next.

How Adolescence Has Changed

As we've said, a century ago observers first noticed the effects of systemic abandonment on development—how our neglect and adult self-interest had created the necessity for a whole new stage of the life span. Adolescence was and is here to stay. Now that we know the *why* and *what* of adolescence, as parents we are ready to dig into *how it looks* and the *what now* of the process. Adolescence began as a snowball at the top of a mountain, and from the 1960s through the early 1990s it has kept on rolling, gaining speed and steam. Today it is no longer a snowball rolling down on society; it has become an avalanche that is out to suffocate us all. Welcome to the new adolescence.

Timing, Duration, and Stages of Adolescence

In the past, becoming an adult coincided roughly with the time of the onset of puberty. Adolescence and the questions related to individuation now commence when adulthood used to begin, at the average age of puberty in a given community.

Remember, adolescence is not in itself a physical or biological experience, though how our bodies change and develop along the way certainly plays a part. The essence of adolescence is growing individuation—the progression leading to a discovery of and commitment to entering the adult world.

For many centuries, *pubertal* (Latin, meaning "adult") referred not only to the biological aspect of adulthood but to the entire package. Once adolescence came on the scene, puberty shifted to simply being about body changes, not about a change in social status or adult competency. Yet puberty, or biological adulthood—or at least the average age of puberty—is considered the marker for when the individuation process begins. And because there is little data to show when the average age of male puberty begins and there is evidence that the female reproductive system somehow adapts to its environment, the average age of *female* puberty indicates when both boys and girls start on the road to individuation. A young person moves out of adolescence when the three questions of identity, autonomy, and belonging have been addressed. Essentially, adolescence begins in puberty and ends in culture.

The timing of this has changed dramatically over the last several decades. In 1900, the average age for the onset of menses in girls of the dominant culture in the United States was somewhere around fourteen and a half or fifteen years old. At that time individuation as we now define it took only a few years at most. Shortly after the Second World War, female puberty began to start younger, and it is generally agreed that by 1970 the average age was around thirteen years old. Through the postwar period and into the 1950s and 1960s, the most significant markers of entrance into adulthood were graduation from high school and getting married, and most adolescents were on their way to adulthood by eighteen or nineteen years old. But during the 1960s, the 1970s, and even the 1980s, adolescence began to last even longer as the college experience became more normative and young people were beginning to wait longer to get married. It was during these decades that the period of adolescence

> Essentially, adolescence begins in puberty and ends in culture.

received more attention—but for the most part it was *negative* attention. Sure, as life got more complex and society more fragmented, some took a few years longer to enter adulthood during those years. But for most of today's parents, adolescence lasted somewhere between five and eight years.

	BIOLOGY Average age of female puberty	**CULTURE** When the three tasks have been settled
Pre-1900	14+	16
1980	13	18

Jump to today, where the average onset age of female puberty has continued to decline.[2] But the big story for adolescents is not that; it is the other end of the equation—entering into full status as an adult has become increasingly difficult and precarious in the last several years. It takes much, much longer than it did even twenty years ago. Today, researchers tell us, the process of individuation can last well into the middle or even late twenties.

The point of all this? What was a sometimes difficult but usually not devastating process when *you* were a teenager has become a thirteen- to fifteen-year slog through the most difficult questions life will ever throw at us, like *Who am I? What power do I really have?* and *Where do I fit?* The greatest challenge of growing up today is to have been born into a society that has encouraged and even promoted delayed adolescence—all without offering anywhere near the support one needs to survive the rigor of this lengthy and isolating journey.

	BIOLOGY Average age of female puberty	**CULTURE** When the three tasks have been settled
Pre-1900	14+	16
1980	13	18
2007	12	mid-20s

For a long time researchers noticed two fairly distinct stages of adolescence, early and late. Early adolescence is that time when although you are no longer a child, you are still a long way from being an adult. An early adolescent can be described as being *concrete* in how they think, how they process information, and how they relate to others. Life is generally black and white, and behavior is based not on reflection and experience but on the immediacy of circumstances and emotion. A late adolescent, on the other hand, is almost ready for adulthood but has not quite grasped the necessity to interdependently insert themselves into adulthood. In other words, they think they are adults, yet they are not quite able to take on the full responsibility of what that actually means. Late adolescents like to gather in small groups of like-minded friends and tend to disdain much if any direct advice or counsel. In contrast to early adolescents, a late adolescent is *abstract* in their ability to think and process information and also in how they relate to others.

The age characteristics of both of these stages have been relatively stable since the early part of the last century. This means that when you were in junior high you were an early adolescent, when you were in high school you were a late adolescent, and soon after graduation you began to transition from late adolescence into adulthood. But as we've said, over the last few decades the landscape has changed, impacting the developmental progression dramatically.

Today there are no longer two stages of adolescence; we now have three. Although early adolescents are still concrete thinkers, they experience an entirely different set of challenges than we did twenty years ago. However, the key identifiers and the progression remains the same. The characteristics of late adolescence, especially the confidence to take life by the horns without too much thought given to their vul-

> The greatest challenge of growing up today is to have been born into a society that has encouraged and even promoted delayed adolescence—all without offering anywhere near the support one needs to survive the rigor of this lengthy and isolating journey.

nerabilities or weaknesses, have also remained the same. But as adolescence lengthened and both early and late were stretched to the breaking point, a brand-new

> The defining characteristic of midadolescence is *egocentric abstraction.*

stage popped onto the developmental radar screen—we call this phase *midadolescence.* Neither concrete nor abstract, midadolescence is the stage of life that is marked by the beginnings of abstract processing and relational awareness, but midadolescents do not yet have the developmental capacity to see outside of their own life and needs.

We call the defining characteristic of midadolescence *egocentric abstraction.* This period usually occurs somewhere from fourteen to twenty years old. During midadolescence your child is striving to be noticed and affirmed, yet they're also a long way from knowing who they are or what personality and gifts God has given them. This is the stage of adolescence that is relatively new, recognized about a decade ago as adolescence lengthened and the early and late stages were stretched to the max. This is an understudied and unique time that kids go through but parents have never known. The tasks and identifiers of early adolescence have remained relatively stable, and late adolescence, although occurring later than we went through it, is roughly the same stage we experienced. So even if your children are years away from midadolescence, every adult needs to know what our kids face as they go through this wild emerging stage of development.

Midadolescence: A Whole New Ball Game

Most parents feel like they understand their teenagers. As often as we profess that high school was great, we can all think of times and seasons when those years were about as tough as it gets. We knew even then that life was not all free and easy and that the way the world was evolving was causing us to feel more and more marginalized. Most of us didn't seem to care, because we were fairly close to adulthood (we were late adolescents then); we wanted to spread our wings on our own anyway, or at least we thought we did. But we did know that something was going on around us, and it was affecting us. From *The Breakfast Club* to *Can't Buy Me Love*, the media reminded us that our culture was changing and we were all trying to figure out how to deal with it . . . and that was twenty-plus years ago.

As we mentioned in chapter 1, the first thing that parents must come to grips with is that the junior high and high school life they lived is long gone. It simply no longer exists. How our children and teenagers experience life today, especially on a "macro" level,[3] is a far, far cry from how we experienced it. This is something every parent *must* learn to acknowledge and face. As we offer this background to you, our goal is to help you understand how deep and wide is the chasm between the adult world and the adolescent "world beneath."

In wrapping up the nature of contemporary adolescence, we want to unpack our core conclusion from the research described in *Hurt: Inside the World of Today's Teenagers*. This immersive study was conducted during 2002 on a Southern California high school campus. In addition, a research team compiled reams of notes from what others were reporting about this age group from around the world. We then followed up with conversations and focus groups with hundreds of kids from all over North America. What we are describing throughout this book are but a few sweeping and summary comments from what we learned. They are not exceptionally detailed, but they do offer a mosaic of kids today. We will sprinkle these observations in part 2, where we will take a look at how each of these (and other) issues are expressed during each particular stage and what our response can be. For now, however, to be able to appreciate what your younger children will go through and to recognize the world your midadolescent lives in, we as adults must all come to grips with one determining reality. It all begins with the community that adolescents claim is the only safe place they have, the underground world where adults are not welcome—the "world beneath."

The World Beneath

During the first few weeks of the *Hurt* study, one distinctive and surprising observation emerged out of the din of our assumptions: once adolescents begin to develop abstract awareness, they realize that others' choices have the ability to bless or curse, and they quickly recognize how wounded they are from the agendas of others. In response, and primarily as self-protection, they grab onto each other and dive underground. This world reshapes their worldview and ethical systems, at least for a season. During this time parents will take a metaphorical backseat to the influence of their teenager's friends. With most kids, at least now and then, the drive to stay close to friends trumps every other basic need they have, including (unfortunately) food, sleep, and self-protection. In fact, the defining characteristic of midadolescence, *egocentric abstraction*, dictates an irrational (to parents especially) loyalty to other kids, even those whom they know are way out there on the edge.

Many adults contend that all of us did this in high school, and we believe that to a degree this has been true for decades. As "youth culture" was beginning to emerge in the 1940s and 1950s, kids and adults could still walk together on the cultural landscape. As the years progressed, the distance between adults and kids became more evident—that youth culture pathway in the landscape soon became a trail, then a ditch, and finally in the 1980s a deep trench. Sure, during those years kids (late adolescents) could climb in and out of the ditch and join adults in conversation and partnership, and adults could now and then jump into the ditch (but even this was usually seen as unwelcome and invasive). During this period lots of adults and adult systems, from youth ministry to educational leaders to the government, were making a lot of noise about the state of "our youth." From 1980 to the mid-1990s, advocates of the young sought to reenergize the adult community's commitment to the young. When Mike Yaconelli, late cofounder of Youth Specialties, pronounced to a gathering of a few thousand youth ministers, "We are losing our kids, and nobody seems to care!" the outrage and determination was palpable. Then, in the middle 1990s, that soul-wrenching conviction somehow faded into the background.

About a decade ago, as scholars started to more freely use the term *midadolescence*, adults stopped talking about the distancing of our kids and breathed a collective sigh of relief that everything was fine, because we had discovered that we weren't "losing" our kids. We became convinced that any problems the young were having in assimilating and feeling connected to the adult community were due to the universally accepted thesis that Generation X had arrived. Now that the societal fragmentation and relational erosion many had seen coming for decades had such an easy and clean solution to ease our conscience, adults stopped worrying. "Our kids are fine; they're just postmodern, generationally defined slackers who will eventually figure it out."

What happened to the kids? Where did they *go*?

To the world beneath, which, by the way, is alive and well and becoming far more sophisticated and protective every year. It is the place they go to find safety and, ironically, rest from the myriad expectations and agendas they have to face every day. In the world beneath, the rules are more straightforward, like loyalty to friends and collective self-protection. It is not quite the Shangri-la that most adults assume it to be, but to the adolescent mind-set, it usually feels like the only place they can let down their guard without being prodded, accused, hassled, or probed.

The world beneath refers to the lone safe relational place midadolescents believe they have left—other kids. It is in this world where loyalty to each other is (usually) the greatest value they have. It is their own world where they do not feel they will be hassled or judged. It is the world where they have their own language, style, music, and, for most kids at least during the midadolescent years, worldview. No matter how "cool" they are, adults are not welcome, because the reason the world beneath exists is for protection

> What happened to the kids? Where did they *go*?
>
> To the world beneath, which, by the way, is alive and well and becoming far more sophisticated and protective every year.

from the multiple agendas that control and manipulate midado-lescents. During this season many parents feel like their children are leaving them behind and want nothing to do with them. But that is not what is going on. They are simply trying, with the rest of their peers, to find a relational place where they can rest and regroup to head out into the high-pressure world of adult expectations. Regardless of how your child behaves, with very, very few exceptions, the last thing they want you to do is leave them. They need you, and at the core they want you.

If you really want to understand your fourteen- to nearly-twenty-year-old child, you need to come and sit on the steps of the world beneath. Invite them to be your guide as you become a student of their world. You can never go into that world, but you can ask them to help you to understand what it looks and feels like. Sure, use MySpace or Facebook or whatever the technologi-cal flavor of the day as a resource, but don't be a detective who is out to "get the scoop" on your kid and their friends. As you go through the weeks, months, and years of leading, guiding, and loving your child, remember—the best possible gift you can give them as they enter high school and move through the last decade of adolescence is the willingness to let them guide you, at least in understanding the world where you can never go.

6

Systemic Abandonment
Or, How Did We Get Here?

There is little or no place for adolescents in American society today—not in our homes, not in our schools, and not in society at large. We have, in effect, all but eliminated this age period as a distinct stage of the life cycle.

David Elkind, *All Grown Up and No Place to Go: Teenagers in Crisis*[1]

"I know when this all started, this adolescent thing—when the Supreme Court took prayer out of the schools."

During the question and answer time of a recent parenting seminar, a father sitting in the crowd of a few hundred parents made this statement to me. He said it in a way that declared the issue was settled, with a thinly veiled confidence and even an edge of anger in his proclamation. The crowd turned as one and stared at me, waiting to see how I would respond. It was what you may call a "pregnant" moment. How does one answer such a comment?

What made this remark so difficult is that it gets at the heart of where we immediately turn when confronted with anything that bothers or threatens us—we want to find the culprit and attack. As we come face-to-face with a rapidly changing adolescent reality, knowing our own kids are going to be deeply affected by it, we feel like we have to do *something*. To step back and carefully examine how we got to where we are and to analyze and dissect the multiple issues that come into play when it comes to raising children in a changing cultural climate takes so much work that it is simply easier to play the blame game. As a front-page headline of the *Seattle Post-Intelligencer* put it a few months ago, "Kids Today Are Spoiled—What to Do." Without a word on the complexity of the problems facing this generation of youth, the lengthy article simply assumed they had nailed the diagnosis and went on to suggest prescriptions for solving the situation. It is hard to blame them, really, because we all do it.

For example, when the day comes when one of us develops some kind of physical ailment that makes us nervous, the last thing we want a friend to tell us is, "Oh, I know what that is! I read all about it on WebMD!" Our instant, microwaving, sitcom culture has seeped into every area of our lives, where we assume even the most complex and nuanced issue or situation can be assessed and solved in mere seconds. With all the information we've been bombarded with throughout our lives, and with the wit and wisdom of the proverbial Dr. Phils loading us up with rapid and omnipotent insight, we all fall into the quick-fix trap of instant judgment. It's in our postmodern genes.

When it comes to parenting, however, this is a serious and dangerous trap. As parents we must remember that the more serious an issue is, the more careful we need to be with our observation, analysis, and diagnosis. In the above medical example, we would not only want to find a qualified doctor to take a look, but eventually we would want to consult a highly recommended specialist, and not just *any* specialist but *the best* specialist. In leading and loving our kids, and being responsible for at least a piece of their developmental journey and future, the last thing any of us wants is to rely on flippant, superficial, or knee-jerk diagnoses that may trip off the tongue because we have heard them so often *but may not actually be right.* We need to sit back and think. We want help in assessing the full picture of what we and our children face today and tomorrow. We want to be able to get a clear and well-constructed analysis so that we are prepared to do the best we can with and for our kids. We all know, and sometimes even admit, that life has changed and changed dramatically. We also know it has affected us over the years. And most of us live in a perpetual state of concern and even fear over how deeply it is impacting our own children. When we step back and really think about the life we have handed our kids, few of us emerge unscathed from a barely concealed sense of foreboding. That said, then, before we move into how to parent in our crazy and disjointed world where adolescence is such a difficult and precarious journey, we need to look carefully at how we got to where we are and why. As with anything that matters, the most effective prescription begins with the most thorough and careful diagnosis.

A Thesis: Systemic Abandonment of the Young

Fancy words—"systemic abandonment." We are not trying to impress you or to somehow give you a "head fake" into abstract theory. We believe that these two words best describe what has happened to our kids. In short, we are convinced that the "problem" of extended adolescence and the creation of the world beneath is due to the insidiousness of the universal yet subconscious conspiracy of the systemic abandonment of our young.

In 2002 I (Chap) lived in and intensely studied the world of kids, and I listened to their perspectives on everything from sex and school to parents and friends. I came away with one general overall impression: We (as "adults," not necessarily as individuals) have hurt our kids. We, all of us, have led our children into an environment where they have never been more ill-equipped to handle the world we have handed them. We expect much and complain much, and yet we listen so little. We demand respect and courtesy, but we are unwilling to return what we demand. In every system and structure, organization and institution, we have literally left our kids adrift in a growing tempest without the power or compass to help them navigate their way around and through the storms that life will throw at them. This impression emerged out of every conversation, email, poem, song, and note we have received from over a thousand kids since we began the study. Not only have the messages conveyed a sense of abandonment and aloneness, but in almost every case they also oozed fragility and pain. Our children have been wounded as a result of our neglect, and what is even more frightening is that by the time they hit high school, they all know it.

This hasn't been an easy sell for adults. Despite the strength of the research and the overwhelming uniformity of adolescents' response to their plight, so many of us still want to dust off our long-developed biases and assumptions regarding why kids are the way they are today. Some are convinced they are spoiled, and therefore we should rein in their access to resources. Others (like the gentleman who spoke up during my seminar) believe the cause is located in the weakening of an evangelical presence in the public square, and thus the answer is to "bring God back into the schools." Most blame the generically applied "breakdown of the family," an important factor in the changing societal landscape, to be sure, but a far-too-easy target to have had this big of an effect on all of society. For these folks the solution is less clear, but at least the evil has been named. And then there are those who denigrate Hollywood, rock music, advertisers, and on and on it goes (did someone say "global warming"?).

In a careful look at each of these hugely important factors influencing culture, each one (and more we haven't mentioned) has obviously contributed at least somewhat to a continuing lack of concern or support for our kids. We believe what has separated us from our kids and caused adolescence to lengthen is not a reaction to any one influence but rather these and many other factors all combining together as visible symptoms of a deeper, even more insidious and destructive conspiracy of neglect by default. If we were to assume that overindulgence and entitlement (as in "today's kids are spoiled") are the reasons our kids take longer to become adults, then we could collectively choose to rein in the opportunities, resources, and finances that children and adolescents have access to, and that would solve the problem. But if being "spoiled" were the primary cause of lengthening adolescence, one would logically assume that this would stimulate a desire for kids to individuate so that they could produce their own income stream to gratify their "gluttonous" cravings. Here is where the logic breaks down, as clearly this is not the case.

Or say we point out that the problem is that Hollywood is out to control or "get" our kids. If that were true, our response would again be obvious, decisive, and potent. As a society we could come together and force "them" to back off and stop making growing up more difficult (assuming that "Hollywood" represents a monolithic community that is more concerned with the demise of the young than with corporate profits).

We are convinced that on their own, *none* of these issues have either the will or the power to create such a massive and irreversible social shift as has been going on for the last several decades. While each of these stokes the fires of the changes going on, they are more symptoms than causes in that they feed off of the changing reality rather than being the cause of the changes. Overindulging our kids; the proliferation of films, television, and music; the expanding technological options; and even the weakening of the family are all indicators of a disease that is eating away at the inner fabric of our life together. We have disassembled our "metanarrative," or communal story. We have ripped ourselves away from family, friends, and meaningful relationships. We have given in to the idea that the only thing to live for is TGIF ("Thank God It's Friday"), where all we have to offer our children is an opportunity to indulge in a favorite leisure activity while we wait to retire. We have no vision, no passion, no dreams—and worse, we've passed on this fatalistic, dismal, and depressing legacy to our kids. We have no idea what it means to live, to laugh, to dance. And we wonder why our children don't want to become adults more quickly!

To see what has happened to cause such a gray forecast, let's briefly look at two different systems, merely as examples, that are verbally committed to nurturing children and adolescents as they attempt to find their way into adulthood.

Sports

During the first few decades of the twentieth century, cities did not have organized recreation programs, and next to nothing was offered to serve this new not-yet-adult and no-longer-child group. In the 1920s and 1930s, adolescents often found themselves with little to do and even less support. In response to this, caring adults began to think of creative ways to connect with and serve these young men and women. One of the most visible that has lasted these decades is youth sports. Take the genesis of the youth football program called Pop Warner.

It all began in 1929 when the owner of a new factory in Northeast Philadelphia enlisted the aid of a young friend, Joseph J. Tomlin, to solve a recurring problem. The factory's huge ground-to-floor windows were constantly being shattered—100 broken windows in just one month—by teenagers hurling stones from a nearby vacant lot. . . . Joe Tomlin, an enthusiastic athlete who had excelled in sports in high school and college, had a possible answer. Since the other factories in the area were also being plagued by the young vandals, he suggested that the building owners get together to fund an athletic program for the kids. In those days, the city did not have organized recreation programs to keep idle kids occupied and out of trouble.[2]

From Pop Warner football leagues to the first Little League games, adolescents were given the opportunity to connect with a few adults who cared for them, who were willing to teach them, and who were there for them.

But youth sports have changed. When we adopted the rhetoric we love to attach to our love affair with sports even for very young children—"sports builds character"—who could have envisioned this looking like it does today, especially for children?

While there is no consensus as to the positive nature of sports for youth development, it doesn't take a psychologist to watch a T-ball or youth soccer game and realize how far we have come from offering the support kids need. What has happened is that we still use the rhetoric of "character" to elevate the value of youth sports, but today character is put on the back shelf at best. What matters now, at almost every level of sport, is that the best get better, the weaker learn how to support the heroes, and sport is only about winners and losers.

The current state of youth sports is an example of how we as a society have abandoned our young. Even a generation ago, sports were important, but only as an aspect of life, not as the central focus while growing up. Thirty years ago, if a high school freshman wanted to try a sport, in most schools they could have the opportunity. Today in most schools the only way to play a sport is to commit to competitive travel leagues as early as possible, just to get the chance to make a team. No wonder by the time kids get to high school now the vast majority have neither the interest in nor even the competitive capability required for participating. To the surprise of few, this is a big reason why so few high school kids care about their school's sports teams—they represent a club with few members, and those who *do* participate are often sick of the sport by the time they reach the varsity level.[3]

As Joseph Doty, a professor of physical education at the United States Military Academy who studies character development through participation in sports, writes:

> Can positive character traits be developed through a sporting experience? Absolutely. But it will not happen by chance or hope. It can and will only happen when coaches, teachers, and administrators make a conscious decision to make character development an outcome (objective) of the sport experience.[4]

That is precisely our problem today. This indictment, however, has more to do with the way we as a society have collectively allowed an entire industry to change how our kids experience life. Clearly more coaches are good than are bad; obviously not everyone who leads and coaches youth in sports hurts them or even discourages them. But we have allowed sports, as a social force and *system*, to lose their moorings in communal interaction and developmental encouragement. Even the most inane youth sport has become just one more adult-driven competition where all that matters is winning and losing. Coaches can be sincere and sensitive to the eight-year-old just learning a sport, but if another kid is more "gifted" or talented, the new learner does not get the chance to compete. As one parent told us, "There are winners and there are losers. They have to figure out sometime which they are, right? And the earlier the better, I say."

We still talk about character, but what we really mean is learning the tough lessons of life through sport—winning and losing, surviving adversity (and for lots of kids that means coaches and parents yelling from the time the kid first straps on a soccer shin guard).[5] What was originally offered as a support out of a concern for children's development and nurture has become more about the success of programs and winning teams. In other words, what used to be about the kids is now about the adults who run the programs—the boards, coaches, and parents. That's abandonment.

Education

In the early years of the twentieth century, we as a nation took high school (or secondary) education seriously. Educational leaders recognized the importance of staying on top of cultural shifts to ensure that our children had the best shot at being prepared to enter the adult mainstream. As this statement from a 1928 federal report on education makes clear, the needs of kids must be the driving goal of our educational institutions:

Secondary education should be determined by the needs of the society to be served, the character of the individuals to be educated, and the knowledge of educational theory and practice available. These factors are by no means static. Society is always in process of development; the character of the secondary-school population undergoes modification; and the sciences on which educational theory and practice depend constantly furnish new information. Secondary education, however, like any other established agency of society, is conservative and tends to resist modification. Failure to make adjustments when the need arises leads to the necessity for extensive reorganization at irregular intervals. The evidence is strong that such a comprehensive reorganization of secondary education is imperative at the present time.[6]

Today, for lots of reasons, it seems as if we have forgotten this central calling of education. We do not believe it is any particular group's fault, although depending on who you ask, you may find plenty of fingers being pointed at the demise of our educational systems, as this widely circulated email illustrates:

Hello! You have reached the automated answering service of your school. In order to assist you in connecting to the right staff member, please listen to all the options before making a selection:

- To lie about why your child is absent—press 1.
- To make excuses for why your child did not do his work—press 2.
- To complain about what we do—press 3.
- To cuss out staff members—press 4.
- To ask why you didn't get information that was already enclosed in your newsletter and several flyers mailed to you—press 5.
- If you want us to raise your child—press 6.
- If you want to reach out and touch, slap, or hit someone—press 7.
- To request another teacher for the third time this year—press 8.
- To complain about bus transportation—press 9.
- To complain about school lunches—press 0.
- If you realize this is the real world and your child must be accountable and responsible for his/her own behavior, class work, and homework and that it's not the teacher's fault for your child's lack of effort: Thank you and have a nice day![7]

When we play this audio clip at our ParenTeen seminars and "town hall" meetings, educators enthusiastically applaud. Parents more or less clap, but more out of politeness than assent. For many parents there is nothing funny about trying to get your kid a teacher who will treat them fairly, *for the third time!*

Let's face it: today most teachers struggle with parents, and most parents don't trust teachers. Then you add the pressure administrators feel from parents and teachers and school boards, and blame gets tossed around like a beach ball at a rock concert. Everybody wants the other party to be reasonable and be more understanding and open. Teachers want parents to help more with assignments. Parents want teachers to be more compassionate toward a kid's temperament and schedule. Administrators want more resources, and the government wants better test scores. Everyone has a solution, because everyone has the "in" on the problem. It is not an *individual* problem, it is a *systemic* one.

A simple question begs an answer, then: What about the kids? Who advocates for them? How do the adults begin to act like adults and make sure we get over our differences in order to look at the whole and make sure we serve them as they need and frankly deserve? In the institution of education, we have abandoned our kids.

The Case for Abandonment

When *Hurt: Inside the World of Today's Teenagers* came out, a couple we have known for years objected (rather passionately) to my focus on the issue of abandonment.

"Our kids aren't abandoned," the mom told us. "I have driven them to soccer games two hours away, given them everything they've ever wanted, and made sure they had the best coaches and tutors so they could succeed."

We know this is hard to swallow as parents. Maybe not when it comes to the larger society, but to think that we personally may somehow contribute to "abandoning" our kids seems counterintuitive (especially for anyone who would read a book like this!). We sure understand that feeling, and we share it. We hate to think that as we have raised our kids we have also been party to their sense of abandonment and isolation growing up. But in reality, we have to admit that sometimes we have. And more important, even with the good that we did with our kids, they are part of a bigger society and larger systems that we cannot completely control.

Take sports, for example. Our kids, and especially our boys, played sports from the time they were four years old all the way through high school. They have had good coaches and bad coaches. They have endured screaming fans and supportive fans. They have at times been good, even great, and have also wallowed in mediocrity and been forced to endure the stigma of second string and game-ending failure. How can someone say we have abandoned them?

When our oldest son was playing soccer in Colorado, he was big and strong and good. He scored almost every game. Since he loved milkshakes, I (Chap) started a little ritual that whenever he scored a goal, he got a milkshake. It was easy because he scored almost every game. It was his reward for a job well done (at five years old!).

When his brother, three years his junior, started playing soccer, he did not have quite the same impact on his team. When our second son was little and played, like his brother, on the same team fall and spring, year after year, he not only never scored, he rarely intentionally kicked the ball. He later went on to be a pretty good defensive football player in high school, but when he was young, aggressive was not part of his vocabulary. Somewhere near the end of his second year of soccer, his fourth season, I noticed a tear slip down his cheek as we drove by McDonald's.

"I guess I'll never get a milkshake, huh, Dad?"

Even as I type this, I feel myself withering on the inside. With every fiber of my being I wanted the best for my boy and to be his fan and encourager. It simply never occurred to me that rewarding one son for something that came naturally to him *at one developmental period of his life* would have such a destructive and painful impact on the other son. And then it hit me: not only had I abandoned the one who never scored by denying him an opportunity to know that at his age sport was about relationships and activity and fun and to celebrate that by regular milkshakes, but I had also reinforced for my other son that he was only able to celebrate life when he happened to perform well. I was, and at times still am, brokenhearted to think of what I had taught my boys in that simple ritual.

You still may not be persuaded how deeply this idea of abandonment occurs or ever affects kids. Perhaps you have become convinced, for whatever reason, that life is about performance and reward and that children and adolescents need to learn how to find their own way and niche. Or perhaps you view your life and your child's life, skill, and effort as commodities and believe only success and accomplishment deserve the notoriety of celebration. Obviously, it is up to you where you land on this. But we would like to encourage you, even if you are the most skeptical parent regarding the root causes of why kids are the way they are today, to at least acknowledge how true this abandonment is for many kids. What this means to you and your family, then, is that although you may believe that your child has not *personally* experienced abandonment, having had a great family, good coaches and teachers, and a supportive community growing up, nonetheless, *they have grown up in a culture where the vast majority have!* One of the strongest conclusions of our study was how universal adolescents' perceptions of abandonment are for them as a cultural unit. Even if we don't see it, our kids do, and therefore it impacts even the most solid and sheltered of kids.

Because you want to nurture your child into a maturity where they are dependent on the Father who loves them and have confidence that they have been chosen, blessed, and called to make a difference in this dark and lonely world, you have to get your hands dirty *now*. Immediate and urgent fears and struggles can easily shift your gaze from the end goal, particularly in the midst of the disappointments and failures you encounter along the way. Do not let yourself be swayed. Let us commit today that we, as men and women committed to the kids God has entrusted to our care, will work to undo the scourge of abandonment. Let us be a voice of deliberate kindness, careful nurturance, and dedicated compassion not only for our own children but for every kid, everywhere.

It begins with you. And it begins at home.

Bringing It Home

Adolescence is the word we give to the new stage of development brought on by the repeated and systemic abandonment of the young. It began in the Western world and has spread throughout the world. Adolescence as a defined stage of the life span is here to stay, and parents need to know how to deal with it.

The key to the adolescent journey is individuation, the process of becoming a unique person or individual. Three basic, interrelated tasks are taken on along the way: the discovery of identity, the acceptance of healthy autonomy, and the ability and willingness to connect to others in community.

Adolescence begins in biology (or, more accurately, at the average onset age of female puberty in a given community) and ends when the three tasks have been more or less settled according to culture's expectations. When adolescence was first noticed, it took only a couple of years. When today's parents were kids, it lasted about seven or eight years. But today it is a long, drawn-out passage that for most kids takes about fifteen years.

Now, what do we do about it? How do we raise our kids to be healthy and productive adults and also help them to become faithful and committed followers of Jesus Christ? That is where we go from here. In part 2 we will be looking at what it means to parent in both life and faith in each of these stages of life.

Parenting
through the Seasons

Life is seasonal. Some of the most beautiful words in Scripture point this out:

> There is a time for everything,
>   and a season for every activity under heaven:
> a time to be born and a time to die,
>   a time to plant and a time to uproot,
> a time to kill and a time to heal,
>   a time to tear down and a time to build,
> a time to weep and a time to laugh,
>   a time to mourn and a time to dance,
> a time to scatter stones and a time to gather them,
>   a time to embrace and a time to refrain,
> a time to search and a time to give up,
>   a time to keep and a time to throw away,
> a time to tear and a time to mend,
>   a time to be silent and a time to speak,
> a time to love and a time to hate,
>   a time for war and a time for peace.
>
>   Ecclesiastes 3:1–8

With the lengthening of adolescence and the wisdom and care that parenting takes throughout these years, keeping this simple but profound wisdom in mind serves us well. For many years conventional Christian folk wisdom has lumped adolescents (and sometimes children) into a fixed category, vaguely described by the term *youth*. With this singular label, thirteen- and seventeen-year-olds tend to be folded into the same developmental mix. If we are not careful and we allow ourselves to fall into this trap as we parent, our assumptions and philosophies of parenting will cause us to miss the real needs of our child at every stage. In providing guidance and discipline for gray areas, from music and film choices to curfew and money, this slipshod approach simply will not be helpful for either our kids or us as parents. Close up it is obvious that there is a monumental difference between a seventh-grade boy and a seventeen-year-old girl. But in a world where so many people say that "kids are kids," how do parents know what their children need along the way?

The writer of Ecclesiastes helps us here: "There is a time for everything, and a season for every activity under heaven" (Eccles. 3:1). That is a vital axiom to which you must hold fast as you seek to provide the best possible nurturing for your child. Because this is an important aspect of parenting, especially in today's world, this section breaks down the developmental journey from child to adult by using the metaphor of seasons. From the tender nature of nurturing a child to the delicate touch of loving an early adolescent to the shift from authority to guide in supporting a middle and late adolescent, during each season of the developmental journey, parents need to proceed with care and caution. Each stage has its unique challenges and pitfalls. At the same time, each season is also filled with passion, joy, and wonder, especially for the parent who understands what is happening.

That's where we are going now—focusing on each of these stages so that you have enough of an awareness of the particular characteristics of each stage. Going through adolescence is hard for all of you, but for the parent who is deliberate and careful, these years are also a gift you will cherish for the rest of your life. No matter where you are on the parent continuum—just starting out trying to find a way to have a weekly "date night" or nearing the end of the road where you are wondering if you have any influence left at all—being familiar with each of the seasons will help you have the bigger picture you need to respond the way your child needs and deserves.

In chapter 2 we talked about the goal of parenting and described it as getting our children in front of Jesus Christ with the desire that he would touch them deeply. That is our ultimate goal. But we also know that we have other long-term goals that we desperately want for our children to reach, like:

- to be an emotionally healthy adult who fosters solid, intimate relationships
- to be a person who cares about others and goes out of their way to show it
- to know who they are and how they are called to live that out
- to live as a responsible, productive adult who is a faithful and diligent steward of their gifts and calling
- to build a family, if they choose, that is a beacon of light and hope to those who do not know what a good family looks or feels like

Every parent wants their child to grow up healthy, solid, and with a deep sense of self and purpose. We all also want them to be kind and compassionate, to care for the needs of those who are less fortunate, and to be trustworthy and faithful with those they encounter. These are good and right goals, and we believe God has these in mind for your child as well.

When pressed, however, for most of us a quick self-evaluation would reveal that we give far more energy and attention to our short-term goals than to these larger global objectives. We know that it is good and right to strive to develop character over the long haul, yet in reality we tend to be more concerned with how well they did their homework tonight or whether they cleaned their room than we are with the big picture of parenting. "Life

is hard enough," as one parent once told us after a seminar,
"without having to focus on the outcome!" (We're not sure this
father quite got what we were saying.)

Our job as parents is to stay on top of the day-to-day realities
we and our kids face. To ignore the immediate needs and issues
in deference to the long-term goals is obviously asking for trouble
down the road. But conversely, keeping an eye on the long haul
and having our attitudes, decisions, and behavior monitored by
the future is equally as important in raising our kids in today's
culture as fixating on the here and now. We need a framework
for thinking about parenting that will help us continue to move
toward our goals as parents *and* allow us the ability to confi-
dently parent every day. That is what the five tasks of parenting
offer—they give us the parameters for parenting throughout our
child's developing journey.

In every chapter of this section we will be taking a look at the
unique needs of your child through the lens of the five tasks of
parenting. Each chapter will also give a few specific examples
and maybe an idea or two that will help you work through what
each task means for you and your child during that particular
developmental season. As you consider what these mean for
your family, remember that if you have more than one child, in
everything you do and in every way you respond to them and
their lives, it is vital that you treat each of them individually.
No two children are exactly alike, and who they are and how
they need to be parented is different for each child, even in the
same family.

7

The Five Tasks of Parenting

Parenting is hard these days; perhaps it truly is, as the saying goes, today's most competitive adult sport.

David L. Goetz, *Death by Suburb*[1]

"Keep your head down . . . watch the back of the ball . . . swing slowly . . . rotate your hips . . . finish high . . ."

Five bits of advice—commands, really. Every time I (Chap) try to pretend to play golf, I cannot stop the voices that remind me of these five crucial tasks that, for my swing anyway, make the difference between hitting the ball down the middle and hitting it out of bounds or worse. Five tasks to keep in mind, that's my golf game.

But golf, like almost anything in life, entails far more than five or ten or more tasks; it is about the coordination of eyes and limbs and muscles and feel. The beauty of the game of golf, especially when it is played by someone who has played enough that the multiple tasks have become a part of them, is a wonder to behold. For me, for now, I need to keep remembering the five tasks.

Parenting is not golf, but at least with this one principle, they are similar. On the one hand, there is no way to reduce the complexity, intricacy, and organic fluidity of "effective" parenting (even *that* is a somewhat slippery notion) to five tasks. Yet there is another way to look at it. As we describe and define parenting according to five broad areas of concern, we might have a better chance at seeing and even approximately accomplishing our goal. To reduce the tasks of parenting to any fixed number is naïve at best, but we have found that by concentrating on these five, we will have covered most of the ground needed to love and lead our kids through today's adolescent journey.

However, we also know that most of us do better with fixed handles and neatly packed concepts. In general, we believe that we need to be more concerned with the overall *art* of parenting, where we allow our love to flow out of us in response to the wide complexity that comes as a matter of course. But on the other hand, we have counted on these five tasks to help us think, pray, and talk through our responses to whatever issue our kids' developmental journeys have thrown at us.

The five tasks of parenting are:

- understanding
- showing compassion
- boundarying[2]
- charting/guiding
- launching into adulthood

Here is a deeper look at what each task means and looks like.

Task #1—Understanding

A dad approached me one morning after a seminar I (Chap) had given at a men's conference. He was agitated, but more than that, he was deeply bothered.

"How can you say I have to be 'pleased' with my daughter? Okay, yes, I love her, because of course I love her; she's my daughter. But, especially right now, she is *anything* but pleasing."

"What I mean," I replied, "is that parental love demands that we remind ourselves that our care and commitment must be granted underneath, and above, and beyond any expectation or disappointment that arises in the moment. To be the kind of dad your daughter needs and to provide for her the kind of love she is desperate for, you have to work hard to let her know that you first *care* and second are working to *understand* that to her life has become difficult, precarious, and probably downright scary. In fact, because you love her, your first and ongoing commitment to her is to seek to understand her world and her story."

"That is easy for you to say," he shot back. "She dropped out of school, lives at home, doesn't have a job, is lazy and sloppy, and mopes around the house all day. I am not pleased with her; she drives me crazy!"

At first the conversation deteriorated from there, but slowly this dad dropped his anger and began to see his daughter differently. The more he reflected on his daughter as a person he had loved for more than twenty years, the more his eyes were pried open to her perspective and pain. Her background was filled with loss and pain, and at that moment she was going through an extraordinarily tough time with school, friends, and even church, where she had been active just a year before. In short, she was most likely suffering from depression, if not clinically, then certainly in her spirit. She did need to grow up, take responsibility, and get her life moving again, but what she needed from her parents, and particularly from her father, was a secure anchor and a nonjudgmental listener. Her greatest fear was being alone and not having anyone who understood her. Nothing she did overtly exhibited that, but the more the father and I talked, the more the light of understanding began to warm his attitude. His first order of business, he told me as he walked away, was to go home and do his best to become a tender student of his little girl's story. When we were done, I could tell that he got it.

Understanding does not mean condoning, supporting, or encouraging our child's behavior, attitude, or even general life slump. To understand, as the most foundational of all parenting roles, is to make sure that your child knows that you are absolutely, unequivocally committed to working hard at taking seriously the reality of your child's life.

Task #2—Showing Compassion

Henri J. M. Nouwen et al., in their book *Compassion*, define compassion this way:

> The word *compassion* is derived from the Latin words *pati* and *cum*, which together mean "to suffer with." Compassion asks us to go where it hurts, to enter into places of pain, to share in brokenness, fear, confusion, and anguish. Compassion challenges us to cry out with those in misery, to mourn with those who are lonely, to weep with those in tears. Compassion requires us to be weak with the weak, vulnerable with the vulnerable, and powerless with the powerless. Compassion means full immersion in the condition of being human.[3]

This description of compassion separates and elevates the word from simply "affection" or "kindness." Compassion is impossible from a distance. It takes movement toward the one who is broken, vulnerable, or weak. Showing compassion, as a key task of parenting, moves us beyond understanding and even a generic sense of care. To have compassion toward our child means we acknowledge that as parents and as adults, we are the ones called to bring ourselves into their emotional and developmental processes.

Many great parents get tripped up here, and to drum up this kind of response is sometimes difficult at best. Sometimes we get discouraged because our child seems to resist our attempts to get close to them. Sometimes we don't think we should show too much compassion when their behavior or attitude needs to change. And then there are those times when, for whatever reason, we just don't seem to have it in us to emotionally engage our child. If that is how you sometimes feel, don't be alarmed. Showing heartfelt, honest, intimate compassion is not something most of us are used to or even very good at. Often we offer compassion theoretically, from a position of either power or analysis. Or we think we can be compassionate at a distance. We convince ourselves that we have compassion, but in reality we haven't allowed ourselves to stoop down and sit on the steps of our child's world. As Nouwen writes, "Compassion is not among our most natural responses. We are pain-avoiders."[4] We agree. In fact, we are officers of PAA: Pain-Avoiders Anonymous. But that doesn't change the fact that we are called to extend an invested and "in it with you" compassion to our child.

Task #3—Boundarying

Whenever we do a parenting seminar, eventually someone will steer the question and answer time toward the topic of discipline. To most Christian parents, the only thing that seems in question regarding the dispensing of discipline is the method or extent (severity?) of our "punishment" when our kids get in trouble.

"When are you going to talk about disciplining your child?" is the most common question. Usually this is framed in a quasi-teachable attitude that says, "Yes, okay, fine. I get that I need to try to *understand* my kid and even work harder at being a *compassionate* father (or mother), and that's all fine and good . . . *BUT, what about . . . ?*"

Somehow we parents feel like when all is said and done, our basic job is to hold on to the stick. We believe that discipline, when properly understood and administered, is among our more central jobs as parents, as we believe we are all commissioned with the charge to "discipline" our kids. Some believe that for us to be faithful parents, it is *the* role we play in the lives of our kids. Now, certainly not everyone feels this way, and Christian circles hold a wide range of interpretations when it comes to discipline. Many parents have lost their kids by indulging them without the benefit of enough parental control to protect them from themselves as they went through adolescence. Others learned the hard way what a firm and rigid interpretation of that spirit can do to a child and to the parent-child relationship. More harm than good usually results from focusing only on discipline. But on some level most of us, though this is probably more likely for men than women, feel like we are not doing our job unless we are firm, almost immovable in our conviction that we must maintain an appropriate modicum of good, old-fashioned discipline in our homes, at least until our child moves out from under our roof.

But what does the Bible say?

Although the Bible contains writings more than nineteen centuries old, it does provide timeless guidance for us in seeking the balance between what we see as contradictory parenting tasks—compassion and discipline. This is true despite the fact that while the Bible is unchanging in its teaching and authority as the divinely inspired revelation, it also remains fixed as a human set of documents written in space and time. Yet God's voice can be heard across the cultures and centuries, and he gives us a pretty good idea of how our Lord views the subject of disciplining our children.

To begin with, it is important that we look carefully at the Bible's original languages to discern the meaning of the words that we most often translate "discipline." The most common word in the Old Testament is *musar* (pronounced moo-SAR), and it is also translated "correction." Either way, the intent of the word is educational, basically meaning we are to help someone change direction, always keeping the intent of a positive outcome as the motivator and arbiter of the method of discipline. In the Greek New Testament, one of the more common terms is *paideuo* (pie-DUE-o), which is usually translated "teach" or "train." This word is used, for example, in Hebrews 12:6 (quoting Prov. 3:11–12): "the Lord disciplines [*paideuo*, "instructs" or "trains"] those he loves." So in both the Old and New Testaments, the concept of discipline is a proactive commitment to correct, instruct, and train someone for growth. It is about restoration and the direction of someone's life, with the outcome of wholeness as its central objective.

A few rarely used words that have been picked up by Christians imply a harsher and more punitive aspect to correction. An example of one of these relatively obscure words is also found in that same verse, Hebrews 12:6: "the Lord disciplines [*paideuo*, "trains"] those he loves, and he punishes [*mastigoo*, pronounced ma-sti-GAH-o, literally "to beat or whip"] everyone he accepts as a son." In almost every reference to any form of discipline, training, and correction in the Bible, the *goal* of the discipline (usually using words similar to *paideuo*) is what God is after, as opposed to the prescribed *fact of* the discipline that necessitates a punishment. Somehow the concept of punishment and what some say is God's call for us to be punitive when our children do something wrong has seeped into our view of what it means to discipline our kids. Somehow we have gotten mixed messages.

Does God want us to focus on instruction and training, keeping in mind at all times our child's developmental and spiritual progress? Or, as some at least imply, does God want us to teach kids how to comply by doling out a punishment for an offense committed? To put it more bluntly, does God want us to strategically work toward the future, or does he want us to dispense justice for the past? To us, once it is framed this way, there is no question that God's call to all parents is to be wise and shrewd stewards of the gift of our children and to therefore be very careful in responding to behavior and attitudes with anything other than an eye toward the future.

That said, what about Hebrews 12:6, "the Lord punishes [*mastigoo*] everyone he accepts as a son"? *Mastigoo* is a very strong term, and at face value it seems fairly straightforward. But, given the context, it is a rather odd word choice:

> "The Lord disciplines [*paideuo*] those he loves, and he punishes [*mastigoo*] everyone he accepts as a son." Endure hardship as discipline [*paideuo*]; God is treating you as sons. For what son is not disciplined [*paideuo*] by his father? If you are not disciplined [*paideuo*] (and everyone undergoes discipline [*paideuo*]), then you

are illegitimate children and not true sons. Moreover, we have all had human fathers who disciplined [*paideuo*] us and we respected them for it. How much more should we submit to the Father of our spirits and live! Our fathers disciplined [*paideuo*] us for a little while as they thought best; but God disciplines [*paideuo*] us for our good, that we may share in his holiness. No discipline [*paideuo*] seems pleasant at the time, but painful. Later on, however, it produces a harvest of righteousness and peace for those who have been trained by it.

Hebrews 12:6–11

The word "punishes" (*mastigoo*) here cannot, based on the entire chapter, refer to punishment as we commonly use it with our kids. The word itself actually means to be scourged, and in the New Testament is only used to talk about being whipped, as with Jesus (see John 19:1; Mark 15:15) and Paul (see Acts 22:25). Scholars do not agree as to the precise reason for this word in verse 6, but the context seems to refer to the "punishment/whipping" we receive as from the circumstances we find ourselves in rather than our idea of being punished. The word is not completely clear, but the context is. With the exception of "punishes," every other Greek word used in this section is the same one (*paideuo*), and for our ears it is better translated "instructed," or at least "trains." What is evident is that discipline *is* important and matters in raising our kids. But our discipline must *always* be administered within the parameters of training and instruction with maturity as the end goal.

Because the Scriptures overwhelmingly refer to discipline in terms of training and instruction that looks to the future, as we have wrestled with the biblical teaching on discipline, we have come to believe that our responsibility toward our children is to provide the boundaries and consequences they need to help them to grow into the people God is calling them to be. We believe that according to the Scriptures, punishment is *not* to be our method, strategy, or response when our kids fail, are defiant, or need correction and discipline. Our view is that the punishment they experience is consequential to their failure and is ultimately the pain they experience as we discipline. Discipline, then, is punishment enough, and we do not need to add to our kids' pain to help them grow.

The word, then, that we believe best summarizes our task in raising our kids through childhood and adolescence via discipline is *boundarying*. Yes, when properly understood and, more important, applied, discipline is important to help our children grow up as people and as disciples. But we can so easily manipulate the biblical concept of discipline so that it becomes a punitive and authoritative form of controlling our children rather than how God would have us administer it, as a form of instruction and training. Thus *boundarying* is the term we use whenever we talk about issues related to rules and discipline.

Boundarying simply means that it is our job as parents to make sure that our child or adolescent is able to experience the balance between appropriate growth through the exercising of freedom and the need to contain immature perspectives and decision making. Consider the process of boundarying like having a horse that you want to eventually teach to roam freely. Because your chief concern, especially early on, is your horse's safety and protection, you first keep the horse confined in a small stall or paddock. As your horse grows and develops, you then move her into a small pasture with a fairly small space to roam around and graze within. As the horse continues to develop, you extend the fence, negotiating with the horse as she is able to learn how to take responsibility for her promises (okay, here's where the illustration begins to break down, but hang with us for just a moment). *When* (not *if*) the horse violates the extended boundary, you as the trainer pull in the fence, all the while making sure the horse knows why the fence is being pulled in and is forced to own that process. In the end, by the time your "horse" is somewhere in their senior year of high school, you should have (in theory) gotten to the point where the fence is down and the horse is able to freely roam without making *really* dumb decisions. (But even then, at least keep available an active underground fence so you can put the old shock collar on when necessary. Don't forget, they *are* still adolescents!)

We will talk more about this in the following chapters, but for now all that matters is that your child is treated with respect, given the power and opportunity to take responsibility for their choices so they can learn how to become autonomous and independent, and yet not allowed to be the one who is in charge. *You* are the one who is responsible for providing the boundaries necessary to help your child grow into the person that God has created and redeemed them to be. Those boundaries, when applied, are the tools you use to help teach your child important skills that will help them throughout their lives, like negotiation, listening, and healthy conversation.

Task #4—Charting and Guiding the Course

It was a beautiful, cloudless morning. Dee was at the helm of her parents' fifty-foot sailboat, the *Miracle*, and I was in the back trying to untangle my fishing equipment from the previous summer's feeble attempt at harassing a few Canadian salmon. After we pulled up the anchor and headed out of the protected harbor with Dee at the helm, she asked me to check the charts as we took off. Thinking it would only take me a minute to finish in the stern, I yelled for her to "just follow the other boats out of the harbor." As I got into the bird's nest of fishing gear, I completely lost track of time, and when the power boats pulled far away from us, leaving the harbor, Dee was beginning to wonder if we shouldn't check the charts. Just as she was turning to yell down to me about it . . .

    WHAM!
       CRASH!
          SCREEEEEECCCHHH!

Our massive, fifty-foot, multi-ton cruising vessel had slammed into and ridden up onto a huge submerged rock that we hadn't counted on—*all because I was so busy doing my thing that I didn't take the time to check the charts and make sure Dee was prepared for what was out there.* Every glass was shattered, the thirty-gallon water heater had fallen onto the engine block, and at first we panicked, sure we were going to sink. It turned out we didn't sink, and the damage was scary but not anywhere near as bad as we had thought at first, but honestly, that scared us beyond almost anything we had ever known.

Without question I was at fault that morning—I should have checked the charts *carefully.* I never should have asked Dee to take the helm when that morning I had taken on the responsibility for navigation. I got busy and distracted, and because I knew Dee and trusted her and we both knew that she knew what she was doing (when she had the proper information), I left her out there heading for a submerged rock that could have been easily avoided. Even though Dee technically hit the rock, *I* was the one who led us into that situation, not Dee.

What has scared us beyond even that experience? *Being parents in a wild, unpredictable, constantly changing, often hostile world.* That morning in Pender Harbor, British Columbia, was eerily similar to what happens in every family, at least sometimes. As our kids grow older we can find ourselves complacent. We get busy, and we get self-focused. We are so exhausted by the time our kids begin to show some level of responsibility and independence that we allow ourselves to think, *They are doing great; I can trust them.* "Just follow those other boats," we say, and then we move to the background, trying to untangle the rest of life. And for way too many of our kids and way too often, we blame *them* for hitting a rock and throwing all of our lives into chaos.

This fourth parenting task, charting and guiding the course, is about making sure that we recognize *all along the adolescent journey* that we are the ones responsible for reading the charts, plotting the course, and pointing out the channels that can help our kids navigate through the turbulent and sometimes dangerous waters of adolescence. This doesn't mean we hold the wheel for them or even stand hovering over their shoulder as they make every decision and turn. Rather, our task is to help them to read the charts of experience, to point out the dangers that lurk up ahead, sometimes beneath the observable surface (remember our rock?), and to help them develop the confidence to ultimately be able to skipper on their own, regardless of terrain. We won't always be right in our reading of the charts, because no parent can claim to have traveled the waters that their child is on. But you do have experience with many of the issues they will face, and because of your journey you have developed some pretty fair sea legs. Your job, then, is to be there as a friend, a mentor, and a guide as they set the course of their lives.

Task #5—Launching Them into Adulthood

It is true, as Dave Barry once said, that your child begins life by taking hold of your pinky, and, to us anyway, he (or she) never lets go. That is the joy and sorrow of being a parent. You love it when they grab on, and it can hurt so badly when they walk away, because in your heart they are still that precious little vulnerable bundle that needs you. In some ways it feels almost unnatural to let go, but that is really the direction of healthy parenting—helping your child to be able to enter the adult world with the ability and confidence to connect as a gifted and valued peer. Launching them into adulthood begins even in the early years of childhood and is complete when they become your peer and your friend.

You have probably taught a kid how to ride a bike without training wheels. There are as many techniques as there are people, but our favorite for our kids was to run alongside of them holding the handlebars, then move to the back holding their seat, and when they were ready, run behind them *pretending* to be holding the seat but actually letting them try to stay balanced on their own. We find a deep satisfaction inside us when our kid moves from training wheels to riding on their own. We also feel great pain and usually some sense of personal blame when, even with you running behind them, they hit those pebbles in the cul-de-sac or on the school playground and fall before you can catch them. Eyes moist, knees bleeding, and nose running, they go flying into the house, screaming, "*Mom? Dad dropped* me on the ground!" A hug, an "I'm sorry," and some antiseptic, and then back out with them again—that's what parenting is all about.

Remember, the central cause of the development of adolescence is society's eroding commitment to training and receiving the young as we welcome and embrace them as peers, ultimately handing off our collective story (or metanarrative) to them. As the decades have rolled by, we have increasingly dismantled the support systems and structures that were originally designed to provide the tools and training our kids need to assimilate themselves into adult society. This trend has only gotten worse, and it shows no signs of turning around—from a macro perspective, our kids have been systemically abandoned by every structure, system, institution, and organization that claims to exist for them. More than ever our children are on their own to find their way into adulthood and to demonstrate that they deserve inclusion in society. Systemic abandonment is the most serious obstacle our kids will ever face as they enter adult life.

That being said, our final task is to do whatever it takes to *launch them into adulthood.* As parents we are the ones who have the heart and the investment in them to walk them through the labyrinth of adolescence and the entrance into assimilated adult community. In addition, this is where we are the primary ones responsible for making sure that as they become adults, they are also firmly planted in the arms of the Father. Throughout the parenting process, there is no real separation between normative adolescent development and faith development. Both are intrinsically woven together and are in fact inseparable. Theologically, God's calling on each person is not only to be interdependently incorporated into society but also to humbly submit to and receive the lordship and leadership of the God who loves and calls them. "Let the little children come to me," Jesus said, "and do not hinder them, for the kingdom of God belongs to such as these" (Mark 10:14). As a parent, then, I am charged with providing the environment where my child recognizes that true life is found in becoming a member of adult society while at the same time finding their ultimate place and community in the arms of the One who lives and reigns as King.

As with the other tasks of parenting, each chapter in this section will offer some perspective on what it means to wrestle with and incorporate this ultimate trajectory in each stage of the childhood and adolescent journey.

8

Parenting through the Seasons
Childhood

Study after study . . . attest that healthy, happy, and self-reliant adolescents and young adults are the products of stable homes in which both parents give a great deal of time and attention to the children. . . . Paradoxically it has taken the world's richest societies to ignore these basic facts. Man and woman power devoted to the production of material goods counts a plus in all our economic indices. Man and woman power devoted to the production of healthy, happy, and self-reliant children in their own homes does not count at all. We have created a topsy-turvy world. . . . There is in consequence a great danger that we shall adopt mistaken norms.

John Bowlby, *A Secure Base: Parent-Child Attachment and Healthy Human Development*[1]

"I *hate* going home," she told me. "Even if nobody's home, it doesn't matter . . . just the *feel* of my house gives me the creeps. Everybody's on edge; no one's ever happy. It's like this big giant downer, you know?"

We wish we could say this conversation with a fifteen-year-old sophomore was atypical, but in fairness we can't. Oh, by degree, maybe. But on the scale of awful to great in our research, her feelings fell somewhere in the middle. Sure, her description of her home in comparison to some kids' may have been a bit extreme, but compared to lots of others, she had it fairly good. The most sobering description we have heard from high school students when it comes to the feel of their home is one filled with an overload of never-ending and poorly communicated expectations, regular arguments and strife, and a general feeling that being away from home is often preferable to the stress of their family. For so, so many kids, home is seen as anything but safe. The other side of this same line of research? Across the board, kids want their home and family life to be their safest and most secure place.

The Tightrope of Adolescence

When we communicate how child and adolescent development works, we use the model of a tightrope to describe what is going on. Since adolescence is the process where a child moves from dependency on their family system toward interdependency in the adult community, when a child hits adolescence, they go across the tightrope where they learn how to be independent and discover who they are as a unique person. Thus, in model 1 on page 103, the left pole represents childhood, with the support and relationships of the family system, the right pole represents the support and interrelationships of the community, and the tightrope represents adolescence. Because an adolescent must discover who they are and learn what it means to develop a sense of autonomy, they have to go through it on their own.

The journey through childhood and adolescence depends on three key factors working together to create the kind of environment and security that every child needs: family stability and safety, maternal attachment, and paternal attachment. As parents we need to keep all three on track throughout the process, but

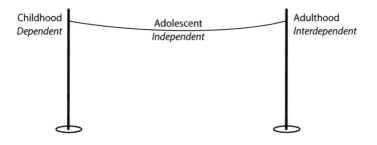

Model 1—*The Tightrope of Adolescence*

during childhood the first two are vital in setting the stage for adolescence. In the following chapters we will deal with paternal attachment.

Family Stability and Safety

In introducing me (Chap) to the congregation as I was graduating from college and heading to seminary, our pastor said, "This is your home. And home is the place where, when you show up, they have to take you in." At the time I felt somewhat affirmed by this statement. But the older I get, the more it has bothered me, for if home is only the place where they *reluctantly* "take you in," then it doesn't feel much like my picture of family. Unfortunately, to many kids and many adults, that is as good as it gets.

After stepping back and considering this objectively, very few adults would argue that family stability and safety are not important elements of child (and adolescent) development. Every adult acknowledges that this need is not limited to children, for every one of us desperately needs to feel like the people that we call family are our biggest fans. The notion of family stability and safety is in essence obvious, so why talk about it? We all need it, we all want it, and we all know it. End of story.

Except . . . unfortunately, for so many people today, home and family are anything but "stable" and "safe." The dark, hidden secret of life in contemporary society is that many people—kids and adults alike—carry around inside of them a sense of dissatisfaction and even despair with the state of their home and family relationships, yet nobody talks about it. Perhaps out of fear that others will judge us, we deftly hide our struggles or push aside those feelings that gnaw away at us and try to pretend that everything is fine, or at least "normal." But perhaps a deeper reason we do not allow ourselves to deal with or even acknowledge our anxiety is that we are afraid that if we begin to explore what we really feel and how wounded we are, we will trigger even greater familial turmoil than we experience now. For many of us, to admit feelings of worry, sadness, frustration, or even loneliness could actually make things worse, because in admitting them we give these feelings power. Once they are named, brought into the open, and talked about, the results could throw our whole lives and the lives of those we love into bedlam. So we hide and pretend that everything is fine. Yet the pain slowly simmers, waiting to erupt at the most inopportune of times.

What few adults realize is that *not* to acknowledge the truth of what they feel or need is far worse than to come clean and go after it. Yes, it can be dangerous to the family status quo to open up old (and new) wounds and risk what you do have. In fact, we are going through that right now with some friends—one spouse has finally "had it" with the other and, out of a desire to "be true to my feelings," has basically cast aside all commitment to the marriage and the kids. But that doesn't have to be the script. You can admit your struggles and pain without destroying those you have promised to love. Just to say that I am hurt, sad, lonely, or frustrated, or even that "I don't like you anymore!" does not necessarily signal the demise of the marriage and the destruction of the family. In fact, the only real hope for a marriage and a family is for the adults to be willing to admit and acknowledge *whatever* they feel, while at the same time honoring the lifelong promises they have made that transcend their temporal but very real feelings.

Some may wonder what this has to do with parenting and why we would bring this up in a book like this. It is because *nothing else matters as much when it comes to being a parent!* Kids, both children and especially adolescents, have very sophisticated radar

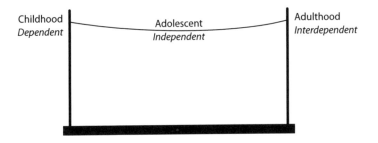

Model 2—*Family Stability and Safety*

when it comes to sensing unenthusiastic, false, or feigned love. We adults have been so jaded by our own life experience that we rarely expect people to truly care all that much anyway. But kids are naïve, and they actually believe that they are *supposed* to be the recipients of nurturing love as they grow up. They can sense tension—even when it is relatively mild and underground—and it causes them to be unsure of their own emotional safety and even worth. Consider the words that flow out of a heart that is free to love—words of gentleness, kindness, patience, tenderness, and respect. These cannot be faked or fabricated. They must flow from a heart that is open and clean and free. Even in a family that has gone through deep struggle, for the health of the kids, the family and home must be a safe and stable place.

As parents we have the daunting and sacred responsibility to be honest, both with ourselves and our spouse, and to pursue the best for our partner with everything we are and have. This is the central and most powerful gift we bring to our children: the willingness and ability to rise above our own desires and needs and give ourselves away to those we have pledged to love for life. In an intact marriage, as both partners seek to "die to self" and live as a servant of the other, seeking the best for their spouse *and* the relationship, the children will sense it and will draw from that lived-out vow when they need to know they have a safe place where they are welcome.

For single parents, creating a safe and stable family life is equally as important, and yet it also can be a challenge. On the one hand, it may be easier to provide the kind of home life where your child knows they are always welcome and embraced. But when you are single and trying to raise a family, issues like loneliness and isolation can cause you to either burden your child with your own painful journey to the point that they become your therapist or best friend, or to expend a great deal of energy trying to heal your own broken heart, either at work, at church, or with your own friends. If you are a single parent, although it can be a lonely, painful journey at times, for the sake of your kids you must do everything you can to take care of yourself while also making certain that the home and family life your kids experience is safe, stable, warm, and welcoming.

Regardless of your circumstances, what matters is that you as a parent make sure that throughout childhood and adolescence, your child is convinced that you are committed to providing the safety and stability they can count on as they attempt to grow up in a world that is anything but safe.

Family Stability and Safety: Putting It into Practice

Ron Taffel notes in *Breaking Through to Teens* that in our society we say and honestly believe that we care about our kids, but when it comes to putting that love into practice, we have failed miserably. As he says,

> The hard truth is that most parents deeply love their children, but they don't protect enough time to pay attention to them. They do not really hear them. They do not really see them.[2]

We have already talked about how marriage impacts this process and what a child needs to be convinced of to move forward with confidence in their own life. But family stability and safety go far beyond just being honest and authentic in your commitment as adults. What kids need, now more than ever, is a family environment where relationships are valued above all else. The way to nurture this, beginning with the youngest children and lasting throughout their growing up years, is by providing a home that is warm and gentle and where the parents are in charge and fun.

A Home That Is Warm

Even more important than creating a family and home that are wild, free, and fun is creating a home that at its heart is *warm*. Studies on teamwork have discovered that to be productive, people need to sense that their team functions within a "collaborative climate." Scholars have sought for years to concisely define what that means. For a long time "collaborative climate" was a fairly fuzzy concept, until a group tested how people view the difference between a "warm" relational environment and one described as "cold." *Cold* relational settings are places and people that people will engage when they have to, but as soon as they are able, they flee. Words that describe a cold environment are *rough, stiff, rigid, critical, demanding,* and *quiet*. *Warm* relational settings are experienced as places people seek out; they want to be there and even look for excuses to be together. Words that describe a warm environment are *soft, generous, accepted, safe,* and *adventurous*. People feel used and unappreciated when it is cold; people feel included and embraced when it is warm.

A safe and stable family is a *warm* family and home. Are your home and family life *warm*, or are they *cold*?

A Home That Is Gentle

As important as parenting is, we would expect that God would say a great deal more about it in the Bible than he does. With two exceptions, where dads are told to avoid "exasperating" and "embittering" their kids (we'll talk about those in the next two chapters), the Scriptures are basically silent when it comes to specific directions on how to be a good parent. There may be several reasons for this, but the most obvious is that this was not an area in which people in the first century needed a lot of specific guidance. Childhood was rather straightforward, families were committed to fairly strict norms for how they hung together, and therefore only the fathers are warned to be careful to avoid discouraging their children. So the next question is, does the Bible give us any hints to help us in a culture where anything goes?

Yes it does, in one of the apostle Paul's letters to a church he had visited in Thessalonica. Although he is not dealing with parenting, he uses the metaphor of parenting to make his point. This gives us a window to peer into the early church's understanding of parenting roles. In 1 Thessalonians 2:7–8, Paul alludes to how mothers treat (or are taught to treat) their children:

> As apostles of Christ we could have been a burden to you, but we were gentle among you, like a mother caring for her little children. We loved you so much that we were delighted to share with you not only the gospel of God but our lives as well, because you had become so dear to us.

The word that Paul uses to describe a mother's role with her "little children" is *gentle*. In light of how Jesus taught about and treated little children, we can have little doubt that in God's economy the most important need of children is gentleness. Some may argue that Paul was referring to women and that men are not called to be gentle. This is simply not a true reading of Scripture—we are *all* called to be gentle. Jesus used this word to describe himself (see Matt. 11:29); Paul uses it for himself not only in this context but also in other letters (see 2 Cor. 10:1), and he repeatedly reminds his readers that gentleness not only is to be pursued (see Eph. 4:2; Phil. 4:5) but also is what the Spirit produces in the life of a believer who trusts in Christ (see Gal. 5:22–23). What children need, then, from *both* moms and dads, women and men, is gentleness.

What image comes to mind when you read the word *gentle*? We picture an old magazine advertisement that shows a huge, hairy, sweaty Olympic wrestler tenderly cradling a tiny infant. This picture brilliantly portrayed strength, comfort, and gentleness in a single image. The secular notion of gentleness being a feminine quality is the worst kind of cultural stereotype, for any man who sincerely follows Christ will exude an authentic gentleness. Men and women both are created to be gentle, and that is especially true for parents. An atmosphere of gentleness is certainly important at every stage of development and is at the heart of what children need from both their fathers and their mothers.

A Home Where the Parents Are in Charge

"How can you say I have abandoned my kid? I have driven her to competitive soccer four days a week for years. She has a cell phone, more clothes than me, and all the spending money she needs! If anything, I'm worried I have spoiled her . . . and now you tell me I've *abandoned* her?"

This is a fairly common reaction we have heard as we have tried to help adults, and especially parents, to understand and have compassion on children and adolescents. Of course, the short answer to this particular question is, "It depends." In this encounter we might respond like this:

Sure, you've done a lot for your daughter. You have worked hard and sacrificed to give her the best you could and to try to figure out the balance between opportunity and excess. But two things about abandonment are important to remember:

Number one, we have been talking about the *macro* abandonment of how society's systems and institutions have abandoned our young *systemically*. That does not necessarily mean that you have specifically abandoned your daughter.

However, number two, giving our kids lots of opportunities, and even sacrificing for them to do and have everything they want, can actually be a form of abandonment.

As a parent, how do you know when what you do is a form of abandonment and when is it good parenting? When you have allowed life circumstances, or oppressive or even destructive expectations that other people and systems put on your child, to cause your child to feel inadequate, incomplete, or unwelcome, you have contributed to abandonment. Any time we allow ourselves to be swept along a culturally accepted line of thinking or perspective that may in actuality hurt our child, we have contributed to abandonment.

A vital aspect of providing safety and stability for our children is making sure that we intentionally and proactively maintain control throughout their childhood and adolescence. In the next few chapters we will be talking about widening boundaries as they grow up, but please do not forget that it is *your call* as the parent to make the final decision regarding where those boundaries land. Your child might, and probably will, fight against your control and will push and press, especially during adolescence. Respecting them means listening to and considering their viewpoint and making sure they know that their input matters as you lead and guide them, but do not for a moment hand them the reins to their life. Although they may not tell you, deep inside they *want* you to be the parent, and that means being committed enough to ultimately hold the reins of their lives until they are ready to take over themselves.

As an example, take youth sports. You have a "gifted" nine-year-old soccer player. You were elated when the recreational coach told you he was "ready" for competitive soccer (as if that is the goal of recreation—to progress to the point of playing with strangers thirty minutes from home and practicing twice as often!—but that's another issue entirely), so you "let him" try out, and he made the team. Now your lives seem to be consumed by soccer—practices, games, tournaments, parents' meetings, hotels, gas bills, missing homework and church, and so on. You feel like you are trapped, but you also rationalize that "this is what our son wanted, so we don't want to deny him. It is worth the sacrifices we as a family are making . . . *especially* because if he wants to play soccer in high school, he *has* to be on the competitive team now."

Who's in charge? Or whose agenda is being fed here? Consider a few questions:

- Does a nine-year-old *really* understand the cost and consequences of playing at the competitive level of sports, *unless the parents impress on him what a "privilege" it is?*

- When he comes home from school tired, kind of listless, wanting to quietly play, or take a nap, or just chill, is he allowed to be a kid?

- Is the cost of missing out on playing soccer for fun with friends one or two days a week during elementary school (or even middle school) worth the "honor" of being set apart? Does the money, time, and sacrifice of church and friends and life *really* accomplish what is best for your child?

Obviously every parent faces these and a myriad of other similar questions with each decision along the way. The point is not to steer you into one choice or another, mostly because *you are the parent, and* you *have to be the one to make the choice while considering* all *the factors!* That is the key for every parent every day: are you willing to say and do whatever it takes to make sure your child has the best possible environment to discover and take hold of the person God has created him or her to be?

A Home That Is Fun

As parents your task is to make sure not only that your home is a stable and solid environment but also that the feel of your home is warm, light, and even fun. How much needs to be written about this? Who doesn't know fun when they see it? Well, according to our research and experience, *most* adults wouldn't know fun if they got hit with a water balloon! In a world that is as dark, lonely, and burdensome as ours, one of the greatest gifts we can give our kids as they grow up is the gift of lightness, joy, and crazy adventure. One of the greatest thinkers of the last century, C. S. Lewis, once wrote:

> When I was ten, I read fairy tales in secret and would have been ashamed if I had been found doing so. Now that I am fifty, I read them openly. When I became a man, I put away childish things, including the fear of childishness and the desire to be very grown up.[3]

Lewis's ability to live out of that free and wondrous place where God's beloved children romp was evident in almost every one of his written works. This is the man who wrote one of the most stirring accounts of the wild, abandoned life we have in modern literature, the playful joy between the newly resurrected Aslan and Lucy and Susan in *The Lion, the Witch and the Wardrobe*:

> Aslan leaped again. A mad chase began. Round and round the hilltop he led them, now hopelessly out of their reach, now letting them almost catch his tail, now diving between them, now tossing them in the air with his huge and beautifully velveted paws and catching them again. . . . It was such a romp as no one has ever had except in Narnia; and whether it was more like playing with a thunderstorm or playing with a kitten Lucy could never make up her mind. And the funny thing was that when all three finally lay together panting in the sun the girls no longer felt in the least bit tired or hungry or thirsty.⁴

We are not saying you need to be a different person than who you are. But we are saying, for most adults, you need to figure out how to release the lighter side of your soul and share that lightness with your kids. As author Brennan Manning once said, "If you know the love of God, and have experienced the forgiveness of the Spirit, and you have been embraced by the Father, then, please, notify your face!"⁵

John 8 records Jesus being confronted with an ethical dilemma. A woman had been caught in the act of adultery, and men who were out to destroy Jesus brought her into the temple courts for sentencing. These zealous leaders threw her at the feet of Jesus and confronted him with what they thought was a no-win proposition: should she be killed by stoning, in accordance with their law, thus showing the people that Jesus was in fact no different from the other religious leaders of the day, or should they let her go free, denying the holiness of God?

Recognizing the cruel scheme, Jesus refused to play along, and he bent down, doodling (as best we can tell) in the sand. His accusers became impatient and agitated, wanting an answer.

Finally, Jesus stood up and made that most famous of statements: "If any of you has not sinned, you throw that first stone" (see John 8:7). Then he bent down again and continued to write.

The drama of that day was not so much in what happened to the woman but in how Jesus took what others had meant for evil and turned it into an act of grace and mercy. When he bent down, he removed the judgmental and violent focus of the crowd from the woman by placing every eye on himself. Although he went on to privately remind her of the danger and consequences of her sin by telling her to stop giving in to sin, while she faced public failure and shame, Jesus was tender and kind toward her.

This is a good model for us as we guide and love our kids throughout their lives. As parents we are charged with a great and honorable calling. It is up to us to set the stage for the rest of the developmental journey. Our task, then, is to make sure that the home and family life we offer our kids is as safe and as stable as possible. To do this means we must strive, from the time our kids are born until they stand tall as adults, to create a home that is warm, gentle, secure, and fun.

9

Parenting through the Seasons
Early Adolescence

You're blessed when you feel you've lost what is most dear to you.
Only then can you be embraced by the One most dear to you.

Jesus of Nazareth (Matt. 5:4 Message)

It can feel like it happens overnight. Just weeks ago your kid seemed to be in a familiar and even straightforward zone, living as the person you have grown accustomed to since they could speak. They were unique from other children, to be sure, but still, as parents you more or less had your kid figured out. Maybe you were one of those who knew what made them mad and brought a gleam to their eye. And moms especially, you might have known what they were going to say before they even knew they were going to speak. Up to the time your oldest child hit adolescence, you may have been among the masses who figured you were one of the rare lucky ones. Others may not have what it takes to be a great parent, but you were pretty sure you had this parenting thing dialed in.

And then, sneaking up on you like middle age, you think you hear a slight rumbling beneath the calm and controllable surface of your family's life. The clouds begin to lazily roll in, the wind picks up a few knots, and you start to wonder if your confidence may have been a bit premature. Then suddenly, out of nowhere, like the midnight lightning bolt flashing across the sky that blindingly illuminates the wreckage left behind by a tornado, you sense more than recognize how your lives are changed forever. The landscape you knew so well and had seen as fairly tranquil and orderly has been blown to bits by a storm. Others had warned you it was coming, but you had no real idea what it would mean. And now that it's here, you can't quite believe that it has happened to you.

For most of us, that's what these initial months and years of parenting adolescents are like. When adolescence hits, it can hit hard, and for most of us it does. Whether you see it in that first major betrayal of trust, or in a noticeable distancing or defiance coming from that kid who used to call you his best friend, or in reading something you wish you hadn't online, you now know that you will have your work cut out for you for the next decade and more. You naïvely had thought that the toughest part of parenting was behind you—loss of sleep, never-ending crying, and an occasional temper tantrum in the grocery store. Yes, there were some trying days when your child was little, but there were also glorious, wondrous days. Similarly, this new season of adolescence is also filled with a wild mix of challenges and victories, battles and hugs, and daydreams and nightmares. These upcoming years are just as rich and rewarding, if not more so, than when your child was small. At times you love it, and at other times you believe you'll never make it through it.

Welcome to adolescence.

When a child enters adolescence, many parents find themselves caught off guard. It is not like we are unprepared, because we all know it is coming. But somehow the innocent wonder and simple logic of childhood that we see in our kids during the elementary years lull us into the belief that maybe, just maybe, our child's adolescent path will be different. Even if it is somewhat less traumatic for you than for others around you, maybe due to your child's temperament or the kind of support systems that are there for all of you, you still will inevitably experience some level of upheaval. The adolescent journey requires some element of crisis; there is no getting around it. No child and their family can escape the necessary shaking up that occurs when adolescence enters the picture. It is no easy thing for either the child or the parent, but if we are ready for it and gird ourselves for the coming changes, we can offer our kids the kind of support and nurture that they both need and deserve.

The Needs and Nature of an Early Adolescent

As we've said, early adolescence begins at the average age of menses in a given community. It doesn't matter so much when your child begins showing physical signs of puberty, because in its essence adolescence is not really about our bodies but about the process of moving from being a dependent child to an interdependent, individuated adult.[1] In our culture this typically begins somewhere between eleven and twelve years old, or roughly somewhere around sixth grade. The entire process lasts for up to fifteen years (or more), and early adolescence generally lasts until age fourteen or fifteen.

Stage of adolescence	Begins	Ends
Early adolescence	11/12	14/15

Among the more puzzling experiences parents face when their child transitions out of childhood and embarks on the road to independence and individuation is trying to figure out how their role as a parent changes along the way. After all, with lots of kids, boys and girls alike, there are times when although they are thirteen, they still act as if they are nine. Yet if you look and listen carefully, you will see that most of the time these child-like behaviors are actually intuitive protective responses that pop up when this scary new adventure may be a little too tough to handle. Nobody can train your child for the journey they are embarking on, and adolescence is really not a natural stage of life as God intended. Add to this the pervasive negative cultural outlook toward our young, expressed via layers of messages that repeat in a variety of ways, "Grow up, kid! Figure it out for yourself. And don't forget, you're on your own!" This demeaning and destructive attitude has made the process all the more difficult. We have forgotten what it was like to be an early adolescent—to make new friends, meet (and please) six teachers, find the lunchroom, and organize our lives to get homework done so we can go to practice. We as parents have to step back and recognize what a wild, crazy, hectic, and fretful experience these first few years of adolescence can be—especially in light of how drastically different life for a middle schooler today is than when we were going through it.

An early adolescent has another strike against them: because they are concrete thinkers and relaters, they do not yet have the developmental capacity to describe what they are going through or even to understand it! Perhaps you've had this conversation after school:

> MOM: "How was school, honey?"
> DAUGHTER: "Good." (Silence)
> MOM: "What did you learn today?"
> DAUGHTER: "Nothing."
> MOM: "Nothing?"
> DAUGHTER: (Silence)
> MOM: "Was it fun?"
> DAUGHTER: (rolling eyes, big sigh, wave to a friend, hide from a boy, then silence, then) "Fun? School, fun?"
> MOM: (after a pause): "Okay, um . . . How about giving me one high and one low?"
> DAUGHTER: "Fine! High, being with my friends. Low, having to tell you what I did at school! You happy now?"

Exaggeration? Maybe. But not all that far off for most kids and parents.

More often than not, parents think that during early adolescence their kid needs and even somewhere buried deep inside
wants to have deep, meaningful conversations. This is true for
most kids, but what parents typically don't see is that we think
we can engage in this level of dialogue *whenever it suits us*. For
most adolescents, communication is all about timing. Especially
for early adolescents, right after school is one of the worst times
to pepper them with questions or try to get them to "relationally
engage." What they really want is to be with someone they trust
will care for them without them having to perform, and even
five minutes of simple conversation can feel like one more layer
of outside expectation heaped upon their already overloaded
psyche.

Maybe you have been trained in the "make a date with your
kids" philosophy of parenting, where we schedule our "one-
on-one" times with our kids. That is a great thing for children,
especially for fathers who find it a bit tough to connect with
their children. If we hear them say that we don't care about
them or don't want to take time to "hang," we whip out our
Palm or BlackBerry and show them right where they are in our
schedule! Sometimes we even vocally anticipate the great time
we will have with them doing something "they've always liked
to do." For you who have done this in the past, before your children became adolescents, these dates may have been fairly rich
times. You see, a child doesn't mind being relegated to being an
appointment on somebody's calendar, for they don't really understand what it means anyway. Before reaching adolescence,
children are generally content with going along with whatever
plans and styles their family system is used to, which means
the parents hold all the cards, pick the activities, and plan the
relational adventures.

However, an adolescent (especially an early adolescent) is
located in a social environment where everybody they relate to
and report to has expectations, an agenda, and a calendar that
the adolescent knows they are responsible to serve. The *last*
thing they want to do is to give up a few hours of Web surfing
or MySpace to go on a "date" with their mom or dad, doing

what the parent wants to do and only when they want to fit the adolescent into their busy schedule.

On the other hand, it is important to remember that your early adolescent still wants and desperately needs that date or something like it. To maintain a good, open relationship with your early adolescent child, this is the stage of life when it is time to let them plan the event, the place to eat, and even the agenda for the time together. Your task is to make yourself available to them with only one goal in mind: to build on the trust and warmth of the relationship. That's it, and that's all. Do *not* use these dates to bring up homework or friends or school, unless that's what *they* want to talk about. An early adolescent will probably just want to do something together, and even though they need to know you want to do what they want to do and are authentically excited to go where they want to go, the deeper issue they are internally researching comes down to this: *"Do you like me enough to hang out with me, even though you probably won't like what we do or where we go?"* Once you can convince your kid that, yes, you do like her enough, then you have proven yourself to be the understanding parent she yearns for.

Traversing the Tightrope

As we mentioned in the last chapter, the best way we know how to describe what is happening during adolescence is the tightrope model. As you can see in model 3, "Needs of Adolescents" (see page 120), when your child steps from the pole of childhood to the tightrope of adolescence, they begin that perilous and precarious crossing of the fifteen-year tightrope. Since the process is really about learning to become a unique person, an adolescent by definition has to move along the tightrope alone.

Early adolescents, who are still fairly concrete in how much they are able to reflect on and see the nuances of life and relationships, don't really know much about what is happening to them during the first few years on the tightrope. They can feel the differences between their life now and when they were children,

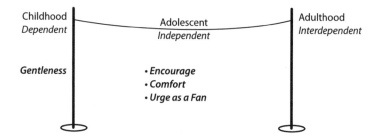

Model 3—*Needs of Adolescents*

and they can even sometimes talk about how life is different. But an important characteristic of this stage is that they do not have anywhere near the abstract picture that an older midadolescent has. As we've said, they may *act* like they want to separate from the family, but they don't; they just need to separate from the *role of child* in the family system. They do know how much they want and need their parents, but they also are conflicted about letting anyone else find out about it, especially their friends.

> During early adolescence, the best we can offer our kids is a sense of security, confidence, and grounding as they prepare to spend the next decade on that precarious tightrope.

What All Adolescents Need: A Gentle and Stable Family

The inherent hunger for a gentle touch never quite goes away even when your child hits adolescence. And this goes for the need for family safety and stability as well. Some parents, and more often than not they are men, wonder aloud if the needs of kids, especially boys, change as they grow older. The assumption driving this view is the belief that young men especially (i.e., adolescent boys) need less gentleness and more training and encouragement in the use of power. Alive and well today is a culture-wide agenda that says boys' primary need is to be taught how to be "strong" and "tough," and therefore they need to learn to fight when they are challenged, or for a cause, or even for a woman. To lots of parents the ideas of gentleness and adolescent boys do not fit well together. To many the advice to "be a man" conjures up the opposite of gentleness and tenderness, and some believe that treating even early adolescent boys with a gentle touch is to fail them by making them soft or timid.

Certainly some kids do need to learn how to summon the confidence to respond when threatened, and this is true for both boys and girls. In a culture and world that demands a certain degree of callousness and formidable inner strength, every child must be taught what it means to stand their ground under adverse circumstances. To treat an adolescent with gentleness, however, is even more important in a world where almost everyone is a potential threat. To help them believe they are worthy of intimacy and tenderness and to till the soil of mercy and kindness, it is far more vital that your child—daughter or son—possesses at their core a soft and gentle response to God and others. Our society is filled with an abundance of violence, aggression, and conflict, and most boys especially are already naturally adept at drawing lines in the sand and staring down an opponent. To help them to live life from a deeper, more caring internal place, they need to be inundated with gentle and tender care.

Throughout their adolescence every boy is crying out for someone to come alongside them offering the gift of a gentle and safe presence. We are convinced that both gentleness and safety provide the critical building blocks, or scaffolding, kids need to move forward with confidence and inner strength. Girls need to be treated with a gentle touch throughout their young lives, and contrary to conventional wisdom, so do boys. In the last chapter we encouraged gentleness with children, and during adolescence it is equally important that you do not stop being gentle just because the world says they need to become hardened to survive. True strength comes from the inside, and that is nurtured and developed only by a gentle, safe, and kind presence. In some cases early adolescent boys may act out their desire for gentleness and safety through destructive or rebellious attitudes or behaviors. As we often tell parents, external behavior never reveals the whole story going on in your child's life. There is always much more to overt behaviors that hurt you or your family. So as you seek to be there for your child, don't be fooled by the outside!

What an Early Adolescent Needs: The Gift of Paternal Attachment

In the last chapter we looked at the apostle Paul's metaphor of a mother dealing with children with a gentle touch as a picture of how he treated those he led in their faith. Later in that same section Paul compares his ministry in Thessalonica to a relationship with a father:

> For you know that we dealt with each of you as a father deals with his own children, encouraging, comforting and urging you to live lives worthy of God, who calls you into his kingdom and glory.
>
> 1 Thessalonians 2:11–12

Again, as we mentioned in the last chapter, Paul's intent was not to teach about being a good parent but instead was to use the metaphor of parenting to describe how he treated those he served and loved. In this case, however, as with the need for maternal gentleness during childhood, we are offered a window into what clearly was the common view of a believing father's role during the first century.

While both mother and father are responsible to provide safety, stability, and gentleness for their children, during childhood the primary person that children rely on is in most cases the mother. The earliest researchers also studied this relational bond that every infant and child needs, called *attachment*, and they labeled the person who was primarily identified as the caretaker of the child the "mother-figure."[2] Today there is plenty of debate about whether a child needs an actual mother or another loving and consistent presence. This is made all the more difficult due to the wide diversity of political and even theological views on gender roles in our culture. What the majority of researchers agree on, however, is that although it is *usually* a mother whom a child attaches to, a child needs both their mother and father to fulfill the basic task of this relationship during the early years of life, and that task is gentleness. The phrase that helps us to understand what it means to care for a child, then, and that describes the call of both the mother and father, is *maternal attachment*. It is not necessarily focused on the mother per se but rather is concerned with how the child receives the safety and gentleness they need.

When a child becomes an adolescent and begins to make her way across the tightrope, she *shifts* her attachment allegiance from maternal attachment, usually focused on the mother, to paternal attachment, most often focused on her father.[3] But even a conscientious and superb father can never be all a child needs, for this again presents an artificial pressure on both a father and his child. Historically, in the vast majority of societies, children and emerging adults were essentially parented by a group of people who functioned in the role that now tends to rest on the shoulders of a father. The need, then, is for *both* a mother and a father, as well as any other adult in the life of an adolescent, to function together to provide what we call *paternal attachment*.

While in the eyes of an early adolescent the father is a central figure in this shift, like with maternal attachment, the mother remains as significant a person as the father. If a father is present but uninvolved, or if he has only sporadic contact with his child or none at all, the adolescent will experience some level of anxiety. A stepfather can be a huge help here, and so can a single mom who is committed to changing how she treats her child, but father hunger is a very real thing that should not be underestimated. Our advice is that when a father has pulled out of your child's life, a careful and understanding watch must be kept to assess the damage such abandonment can cause. Like with any trauma, if you sense any behavior or attitude that concerns you, please get immediate counseling help (and in our recommendation this should almost always be from a state-licensed therapist you have checked out and trust). For reasons we cannot completely know, God has designed us to need the attention and support of our mothers and our fathers. Any loss in this area demands an attentive response.

The hallmarks of paternal attachment? This is where the apostle Paul helps us. During adolescence what we have to offer our kids is the kind of attachment that is encouraging and comforting, and a fan's positive urging to be the person that God has created and redeemed them to be.

What does this look like? We witnessed a powerful example of this before the Notre Dame–University of Washington football game in the fall of 2005. Great anticipation hung in the air as Washington's new head football coach, Tyrone Willingham, came onto the field with his players after having been let go by Notre Dame the previous winter. While the teams were stretching, our focus was on Coach Willingham as he led his team through the pregame routine. In the middle of the warm-up exercises, he began to do something we had never seen before. As the players were sitting down stretching in neat rows across their side of the field, the coach approached each player with a casual, no-hurry air—starter and scrub alike—whispered in the player's ear, shook his hand, and patted him on the helmet or shoulder pad as he walked to the next player.

They lost the game, but during those few minutes this new coach had clearly won the respect, loyalty, and more important the trust of his players. That's what it means to encourage, comfort, and urge on your child. That's what paternal attachment is all about. During adolescence your child needs you to be that kind of a coaching presence. In fact, we all need that kind of coach!

The first two words of Paul's description of a father's role—to encourage and comfort—need no explanation, for they are so central to expressing compassion that we all know them when we see them. The last one, however, where Paul says he treated them like a father in "urging you to live lives worthy of God" (1 Thess. 2:12), needs to be unpacked. The way most of us see the concept of "urging" is akin to the urging of a passionate Little League coach who cannot help but shout to each kid, "Stay focused in there. Keep your head up. Keep your eye on the ball." Some kids may respond well to that kind of approach, but most are undone by the intensity of the coach's enthusiasm rather than experiencing the freedom that comes from being encouraged and feeling believed in. Lots of kids actually lose concentration under this kind of coach because they are so intent on not letting him down that they cannot possibly be loose enough to perform to the level they are capable of.

Just think how easy it is to come alongside your son or daughter and, thinking you were helping them, follow the injunction to urge them "to live lives worthy of God" by pushing them to *perform* their faith as they would a test or a sport. This is not what Paul had in mind. The idea of "urging" in this context is a regular and continual message that empowers your child to keep moving against all odds. It is an urging that instead of tightening them up to live life from the outside, lets them learn how to freely live their faith *from the inside out*. We believe that parental urging is not the urging of annoyance or even a top-down "challenge" for our kids to rise to but instead is the consistently encouraging and confidence-inducing urging of a loyal and devoted fan. This is a fan who believes in their hero, even when all logic would say to give up. That is what our kids need during adolescence—not only encouraging and comforting words, attitudes, and actions but also to be fundamentally convinced that we believe in them.

Your kid needs you to be a *fan*! And not only you but all who are called to love your child during their adolescence.

Boundarying, Charting the Course, and Launching Them into Maturity

For an early adolescent, who is still mostly concrete in their ability to reflect on life and relationships, parents need to kick into high gear the process leading to independence and individuation. Knowing that this is a long process, at least ten years and usually more, our call is to strategically train (a more theologically appropriate word for the biblical idea of "discipline") our child to take responsibility for their own life and choices. At the same time, they are beginning that perilous and precarious journey of discovering who they are. Add to the mix the third aspect of adolescent development, the need to *belong*, and you have the perfect storm of the struggles associated with the adolescent course. Our job as parents is to help our kids do the best they can with the discouragement, confusion, and complexity that comes along with this threefold journey.

> Three fundamental roles can guide you to be the kind of understanding and compassionate parent your early adolescent child needs: a listener, a guide, and a negotiator.

Three fundamental roles can guide you to be the kind of understanding and compassionate parent your early adolescent child needs: a listener, a guide, and a negotiator. If you will keep these three roles in mind in every interaction and dealing you have with your child, you will be able to build into your relationship a level of trust and respect that will make a huge difference down the road. What most parents of early adolescents fail to recognize is that you are not only dealing with the here and now—what your child wears, who they spend time with, how they treat you and their siblings, grades—you are setting the stage for how you walk together when the stakes get far, far higher in the later stages of adolescence. It may feel like that battle over their hair or hat is intensely important, and if you feel strongly enough you will probably be able to "win" at almost every turn. But if you take this same strategy with a sixteen-year-old when talking about friends, alcohol, or sex, you will almost certainly lose. Now is the time to set the stage for tomorrow's more serious issues.

A Listener

Few adults have the patience to truly listen to an early adolescent. Look around you—in a mall, at a ball game, at a restaurant. Parents, and everybody else, virtually ignore children, and it is even worse when they enter adolescence. Some adults are simply clueless and may not realize the impact their neglect has on kids.

Yet we are all without excuse, for what adult likes to be ignored or easily dismissed or interrupted? This systemic indifference to our young seeps deeply into the souls of our kids to the point that by the time they are midadolescents, they are convinced that no one authentically cares. As parents called to lead and nurture our kids, we have to strive to be different.

When it comes to training and nurturing our early adolescent children when they need our leadership, we have to remember that we hold all the cards. We may not feel like it, especially when we feel like we have been taken advantage of or our kids have basically ignored us or the boundaries we have erected. But the fact is, we do have all the power we need to lead our children, especially during the early adolescent years. When it comes to conflict and communication, we control everything from the content of the discussion to the tone of the discourse to the outcome of the argument. This greatly elevates our responsibility to learn how to listen whenever we need to erect or alter boundaries or to help guide their life and decisions.

To listen means to let go of our agenda, at least at first, and to do all we can to try to get inside the head and heart of our child. We need to be adept at reading their eyes and at listening for the logic that guides them, as twisted or ignorant as it may appear (especially when they have made a fairly significant mess of things). In our case one of us (Dee) knows to constantly remind the other (okay, that's Chap) that the first place to start with any problem or issue is by asking questions. We are convinced that most kids—make that almost every kid—will lie when they think they may be in trouble. The skill of listening is to try to create a climate of trust and understanding that will allow the truth to come out. With your early adolescent child, this is really the most important goal. If you are able to establish this kind of willingness to listen to your child while making sure they understand that you need to know the truth to be able to decide together how to deal with whatever brought you to the table, you will have a great foundation upon which to build when they are a midadolescent. So for now, be a great listener.

A Guide

Although your child may be "only" twelve or thirteen, we believe it is imperative for you to make the shift in how you approach them from being an authority to being a guide. You are still captain of their ship, but since the goal is to hand them the wheel and even the compass over the next few years, they need to know that you see them as capable of eventually making their own decisions. This is the second arena that calls for you to be deliberate and countercultural in how you lead and love your child. You need to allow them to occasionally take the helm and steer the ship.

In order to be a fair and responsible guide, you need solid information, and that is what being a listener is about. Now, as a guide, your task is not to tell your child where to go or to inform them of how they violated a rule or let you down but rather to do your best to get them to recognize and then admit the infraction themselves. Your role is to stay at the table until your child sees the issue as it is, even if you need a few time-outs along the way to ease emotional tensions and calm yourselves down. Most of the time you will need to prompt them or connect some of the dots, but the best way to be a guide is to lead them to discover for themselves what happened, and why, and what needs to be done in the future.

A Negotiator

Once you have convinced your child that you care and understand, you have proven your commitment to walk with them with compassion, and you have helped them to comprehend and own their transgression or poor decision making, you are ready to help them to face the consequences of their action. Most parents simply impose sanctions that are usually punitive and yet rarely make much of a dent in what caused the problem in the first place. Often our knee-jerk reaction is to let our kids know how badly they disappointed us and to punish them accordingly. In some cultures this is done by removing a child from the family, using distancing as a training device. In the United States we usually make them stay home (we call it "grounding"). However your family handles "discipline" and consequences, the most common form of adult punishment is to make our kids feel bad, shaming them into changing their behavior and ultimately life trajectory.

We do not think that this approach, as widespread as it is, works. In fact, in the case of adolescents, it can easily backfire. We suggest that you first thoroughly unpack the event that led you to feel the need to impose consequences. First, listen to your child and help guide them into admitting and acknowledging the infraction. Next, work with them to bring to light the contributing circumstances and thinking that caused the problem and why. Lastly, require them to be members in the process of determining the consequence of their behavior. Whatever the offense, do your best to keep them at the table until they come up with a suitable plan that you both agree on. If the issue is skipping classes, then walk through every angle of the issue you can, while not allowing them to disengage from the process of restitution and behavioral change. Keep in mind that it is important to establish a monitoring process to ensure that what you decided actually happens. If it doesn't work or doesn't happen, then you come back together, discuss it, and decide on an alternate course of action. In this way, with any issue, you are still teaching them with respect and compassion that everything they do in life will affect others, and you are training them to see that when they have created a problem, they have to be part of the solution.

Building the Scaffolding for a Lifelong Faith

In helping our early adolescents to take their faith seriously, we need to adjust our strategies and our expectations of what a "faithful" adolescent looks like. During this stage of adolescence, remember, your child sees the world, thinks, and deals with others (including God) in concrete terms. In terms of faith, it is relatively easy to exploit that by reducing the wonder of the call of God on their life to a series of instant platitudes, superficial answers, and content-driven, rote parroting. This is not to say that memorizing Scripture is not helpful, for it is something valued throughout the history of God's people ("I have hidden your word in my heart that I might not sin against you," says Psalm 119:11). But just having our kids memorize Scripture does not necessarily guarantee that they will eventually serve the God of that Word. You could undoubtedly cite numerous examples of how such a parenting strategy produced the opposite of what parents intended. So what do early adolescents need in order to have their hearts and lives softened toward the Lord? How do we help our kids on their journey with Christ while they are in this season of their young lives?

We would like to offer the following list of five faith-building strategies that will till the ground of their souls while they are beginning their adolescent journey.

First, create an environment where faith is "felt" more than "learned." For an early adolescent, emerging faith is more energized and empowered by the consistency of the surrounding "feel" of faith than it is by teaching abstract content.

Second, teach and train theological content, but recognize that you are primarily seed-planting. During this stage scriptural concepts, Bible verses and stories, and theological categories are important seeds that can dive deep into the inner reaches of your child's soul. These are often used by the Holy Spirit in drawing your child to an understanding of who God is, especially as they begin to move more toward an abstract and owned personal faith. However, the seeds that produce the most fruit are those that are planted in the rich soil of the meaning behind the words and phrases. Verses about King David will have a much greater impact when they understand his passion for God and his brokenness over his sin. Avoid superficial platitudes, but rather seek to invite your early adolescent into the more mysterious and messy nature of God's revelation.

Third, provide experiences that connect abstract faith to hands-on relationships and service. Do things together as a family or as a parent one on one with your child, and make sure you use the event to be a teachable moment for communicating the gospel. The mutual and respectful conversation you share with a homeless person while eating at a shelter is what will create in your child a compassion for the downtrodden, broken, and lost.

Fourth, authentically model your faith as consistently as possible. To an early adolescent, you are their Bible. Your lived-out theology—how you talk about people, faith, politics, money, or church—will be the word that your child will study and learn from the most. The old adage "Christianity is not taught so much as it is caught" is never truer than during early adolescence.

Lastly, do whatever it takes to build an extended Christ-centered family around your child. You were never intended to love and lead your child to Jesus Christ alone. It is the responsibility of Christ's body to care for the children. In our culture we have deified individualism so much that we have come to reduce our faith to believing the "right" things, showing up to a big meeting (called "church"), and going about our business, alone and independent. This is *not* the faith of the Scriptures. Find ways to encourage other adults to invest in the life of your child, and your child will see that with faith comes a family.

Faith-Building for Early Adolescents

1. Create an environment where faith is "felt."
2. Be a seed-planter.
3. Connect abstract faith to hands-on service.
4. Authentically model your faith.
5. Build an extended Christ-centered family.

10

Parenting through the Seasons
Midadolescence

It is a wise father that knows his own child.

William Shakespeare

Your children tell you casually years later what it would have killed you with worry to know at the time.

Mignon McLaughlin, *The Second Neurotic's Notebook*, 1966

"High school is different today," he began, but the seasoned teacher didn't stop there. "I'm not sure why, or even how, but—and *you tell people this*—it *is* different today, even from ten years ago. I've been teaching and coaching for twenty years, and there is no comparison!"

All this sprung from a casual comment I (Chap) made in the teacher's lounge in the middle of my research study. "I am asking kids to tell us what they think about anything and everything and why they feel the way they do," I told the small group at my table. "I'm trying to find out if things are different today than they used to be."

His energy-charged comments spawned a lively debate that raged for a half hour, when we all had to go back to class. But the force of his words and the consensus they evoked has stayed with us. We are convinced that the teacher was absolutely right, and yet how life is different, and especially what it means for parents, is what really matters. We have come to see that the most important change in today's adolescence is the creation of a new stage of life known as *midadolescence*.

Understanding and Showing Compassion—A New Term, A New Phase

Stage of adolescence	Begins	Ends
Early adolescence	11/12	14/15
Midadolescence	14/15	19/21

Our conviction is that it is impossible to understand our kids, and much less parent, in today's culture without taking into account the reality and uniqueness of this brand-new stage of the process. As we've said, early and late adolescence have been with us for several decades, but as they both were stretched as adolescence lengthened, they reached the point where neither could be stretched any further. Somewhere in the middle 1990s, this created a whole new developmental stage of life we call midadolescence.

When your child enters midadolescence, the most significant change you will notice is the shift from a *concrete* consciousness of the world around them to a more nuanced *abstract* awareness. During midadolescence they develop a cynical view on authority and a distrust of adults and the systems and structures they control. Most kids say they have been hurt by the multi-leveled complexity of expectations that have constantly hounded them since they were children. You may not have seen this or even agree with their perspective. But regardless of what you think about your child's life and world or how you perceive their environment, to be invited to even come close to them through these years, you have no choice but to work hard to understand and not argue with their perceived reality. This chapter, then, addresses the uniqueness of this stage by looking at how the adolescent community has responded to their perception of abandonment, what a midadolescent longs for in the midst of the process, and how to create a developmentally appropriate strategy for spiritual maturity.

As societies around the world have become increasingly fragmented, with everybody pushed and pulled in multiple directions, there has been a subtle yet steady erosion of our collective commitment to proactively assimilating our children and adolescents into adult society. This culture-wide lack of intentional support and guiding nurture has created an innate insecurity in the souls of our kids.

How a Midadolescent Responds to Systemic Abandonment

In chapter 6 we talked in general about systemic abandonment and especially how it has contributed to the lengthy and isolated process that adolescence has become. We described how as societies around the world have become increasingly fragmented, with everybody pushed and pulled in multiple directions, there has been a subtle yet steady erosion of our collective commitment to proactively assimilating our children and adolescents into adult society. This culture-wide lack of intentional support and guiding nurture has created an innate insecurity in the souls of our kids. From a very early age they are basically on their own to become an adult, and intuitively each one senses this. By the time they become more able to think and relate abstractly and reflectively, they begin to recognize the general pattern of neglect they have known their whole lives. As they recall those messages and events that they see as having been out to get them since they were small, they soon become jaded and suspicious to the point where they may feel that even the nicest adult may eventually turn on them.

These are examples of the kinds of experiences and memories that midadolescents have shared with us:

- the coach who yelled at the clumsy eight-year-old for not getting the catcher's equipment on fast enough
- the teacher who taped the talkative first grader's head to his desk to get him to shut up
- the Sunday school teacher who kicked the girl out of the class on Jesus's love because she was chewing gum and playing with her hair
- the parents who forced their kids to lie to their friends, neighbors, teachers, and even extended family members about the divorce they had lived under for years while growing up

These represent a small sampling of the hundreds of stories we have heard directly from kids. In conversations with them, we simply asked what they wanted adults to know about them and how they were feeling about life. With few exceptions, once they got going, their rhetoric turned angry, frustrated, and combative. Story after story of some event, attitude, or behavior of an adult who was supposed to know better poured out of them. Some may seem minor to many of us (e.g., the irate coach) and others heart-wrenching (e.g., the secret divorce). Most occurred years ago, but to the kids we have talked to, the cumulative effect has been devastating.

What makes this stage so unique is this newfound ability to reflect on both the pain of the past *and* the duplicity of the perpetrator. This is the central thing that we discovered about midadolescents: they can now see life outside of themselves, and yet they are emotionally drenched, both as individuals and corporately. In groups, as one student would open up, another would jump in, sensing a safe audience, and the dump was on! Recently experienced feelings of powerlessness, betrayal, and pain blasted out of them like an ignited fuel truck. As a result of the deluge of hurtful and disempowering experiences they have endured, they feel the need to run from any perceived threat as hard and as fast as possible. That is what the world beneath, mentioned in chapter 6, is all about.

We have found a mixed reaction to all of this from adults. Some can see it and want to do something. Others, for a variety of reasons, have little compassion on what adolescents say about their lives and think they are spoiled and should "get over it." Whatever your reaction to or viewpoint on how today's teenagers describe themselves and the world they have inherited, one thing is certain: adolescence is a longer and more painful journey than it has ever been. Most of us do not expend the energy or take the time to ponder the devastating nature of lengthening adolescence. The fact is that for the last thirty or so years, adolescence itself, and the perilous nature of the journey, has made its mark on all of us who have gone through it. Nearly all adults, hoping to avoid having to face our own cauldron of emotion left boiling from the unresolved issues of our own adolescence, often do not have a great deal of empathy for the perceived pain expressed by midadolescents. At a break in a community ParenTeen seminar, one dad said to us, "They just need to grow up. Sure, life's tough, but kids just need to realize that life is what you make it!" He then neatly slipped into that smug yet ignorant adult fallback position that destroys any hope of understanding, much less compassion: "When *I* was a kid . . ." Arrgggh!

Egocentric Abstraction: The Defining Characteristic of Midadolescence

What many adults fail to realize is that along with lengthened adolescence comes this new middle stage of the process.[1] Early adolescence, described in chapters 5 and 9, could only extend until the cognitive ability for abstract thought and reflection was developed. Over and over this has been shown to be the single most significant marker in the shift out of early adolescence into midadolescence. In the same way, as we will see in the next chapter, late adolescence is the stage where an abstract ability to reflect on life and relationships and process information has developed. But late adolescence, like early adolescence, cannot extend for too many years. The ability to think outside oneself and have an awareness of how my life impacts others and vice versa is what creates the groundwork that prepares and propels one into finally accepting the responsibilities of adulthood.

As adolescence lengthened, something had to give. What spawned midadolescence is the developmental reality that the early and late phases of the process could only stretch so far. A midadolescent is no longer concrete in their thinking and relationships and is therefore able to reflect upon how they affect others and others affect them. At the same time, the length of the journey has created a holding zone where they are years away from identifying who they are and knowing how to exert autonomy. Therefore, during this middle stage, while they have the capability for abstract thinking and relationships, they feel so alone and vulnerable that they are forced into an *egocentric abstraction* that is the defining characteristic of midadolescence. Late adolescents are able to recognize things that contributed to the impact of another's words or behavior toward them, like an angry parent just having a bad day, or a gruff but lonely and insecure coach, or a kind but harried teacher who is prone to overreacting. Midadolescents, however, have neither the developmental ability nor the life training to recognize the nuances and complexities that come with life in a fallen world.

Midadolescents are *neither* concrete in their thinking and re- flection *nor* able to objectively process the multiple factors that have to be taken into account as we learn how to accept and evaluate others, warts and all. The midadolescent, remember, is smack in the middle of the tightrope, where they know there is no going back to the safety of childhood, yet the end of this transitional journey is not in sight. Add to that developmental placement the newfound ability to recall and reflect on the many different people and systems they have trusted and that have let them down. The words that are consistently used by midadolescents to describe their experience are *abused, manipulated,* and *used.*

The consistent reporting of this feeling of abandonment and hurt was surprising to us at first, but then the overwhelming universality of it led us to a more cohesive epiphany: the late adolescent ability to abstractly deal with the world is not a fully developed skill for the midadolescent. They have the ability to think and reflect on life and others, but they do not yet have the ability to *rise above* the immediacy of their experience. The pain is so raw, the daunting nature of the lengthy task before them so discouraging, and the intense sense of aloneness and vulnerability so palpable that the only way a midadolescent can deal with their life experience so far is through *egocentric abstraction.* To be blunt, a midadolescent is at least somewhat aware that their life impacts others even as others impact them, but *they don't have the resources or energy to care.*

> The pain is so raw, the daunting nature of the lengthy task before them so discouraging, and the intense sense of aloneness and vulnerability so palpable that the only way a midadolescent can deal with their life experience so far is through *egocentric abstraction.* To be blunt, a midadolescent is at least somewhat aware that their life impacts others even as others impact them, but *they don't have the resources or energy to care.*

To understand your midadolescent child, and then to show compassion, and finally to apply the boundaries needed to both protect and lead them, you have to become a student of their world. As adults we see a teenage world out of control. We so quickly focus on the outside, and with our kids we try our best to plug the holes in the dam as fast as we can, all the while nervous that the whole thing could soon collapse on top of us. But, in staying with this metaphor, a far better strategy is to put in a few temporary plugs while we spend our time and energy on the dam itself. Sure, the midadolescent teenage world has been ravaged by the dismantling of innocence and anything even resembling the sacred. We observe in their world precisely what we have handed them—rampant sexuality, little respect for others, relational lawlessness, and a general "us against the world" apparent arrogance that not only characterizes our culture at large but also causes adults to fear and flee kids. But you know better, especially if you have been tracking with us in this book. If adults would but look closer at who our kids are and listen more carefully to what they are saying, we would find that what we have been led to assume does not approach the deeper truth that lies just beneath the observable surface. The moral and ethical issues that today's kids face (without enough adult support and careful nurturing guidance) are important and at times highly dangerous. As society stands above and beyond them, critically folding our collective arms while debating the dismal state of our young, we parents need to remember that our default commitment must be to engage and embrace them as we build bridges across the generational chasm. Our first and last calling as parents is to understand as much as we can about their world and how they feel and then to sit on the steps of their world beneath, offering the tenderness and mercy of a compassion that few have felt or even known. This is the joy, and the heartache, of parenting midadolescents in a world that has left them behind.

Boundarying, Charting the Course, and Launching Them into Maturity

To know when to move in and engage and when to pull back and allow your child to live their life is the dance every parent has to learn. No book can teach you how to know when your kid is telling the truth, or fudging the facts, or even flat-out lying. Only you can read the signs, and most of us get them wrong a lot. You are the one who has to learn to decipher the messages to learn which are a manipulative attempt to get their way and which are an authentic "I need you to help me through this" appeal. When they violate a rule or get into big trouble, your role is to bail them out while trying to make them learn from the experience. This is a tough season of life for both you and your child. You can be sure that they sincerely want to love you, and deep inside they probably (mostly) want to please you, but the pull they feel from friends and longings and life itself will cause even the best of them to do something that they know will hurt you. Few kids want to hurt their parents, unless a parent (or someone else) has done something that makes the kid feel like they have no choice but to lash out. They know that their lives are filled with wild, unbridled, and often unexplainable contradictions, yet they can't see a way out of the dark cave that they are in. This is the essence of midadolescence.

Despite all this, your child will need you to stay as consistent and available as at any other time in their life. Rarely will they admit it, even to themselves, but they desperately need you in their lives. For a very few the years fly by without much conflict or heartache. But for most kids, and therefore for most parents (at least the ones who care), midadolescence brings multiple layers of crisis and struggle. Of course it also brings good and joyous times and great opportunities to explore life and faith together as a family. The wild ride of these years is what makes this season such a crucial time in their young life. The choices they make and the patterns they establish may stay with them for years. Both parents and children need to keep their wits together, and parents need to be the rock of security when all else falters.

Your job, then, is to keep building on what you have been doing during the last few years—listening, guiding, and negotiating. If you have done a fair job of consistently working through issues and life with your child through the early adolescent years, then in the next stage you will be able to step into a more adult-like interaction with them that fits where they are in terms of their development. During midadolescence your role is to be a student of your child and their world, maintain a commitment to dialogue and discussion, hold onto your role as the adult, and be reasonable.

Be a Student

Although we have talked about this throughout this book, during midadolescence being a student of your child and their world moves from suggestion to necessity. For so many reasons, what you hear and see from your child and what is really going on inside and around them are most often not the whole story. Way too many parents allow themselves to get so busy and caught up in their own lives that they fly across the surface of their child's life. Then when a major blowup or episode occurs, the parents are completely caught off guard and unprepared to handle the fallout. During midadolescence, being unaware of what is going on with your son or daughter at school, with friends, with sports and other activities, and even in their private life is inviting relational, emotional, and sometimes financial disaster. We know and we have been there in all three areas.

To do your homework with your child during high school, and even the first year or two out of high school, means that you need to be watching and listening for the cues and clues that will help you to know what they are dealing with. Take friendships, for example. For most of us, in high school we had a couple of good friends, and we generally also had a much larger group where we felt more or less comfortable and accepted. Today, due to the complexity of midadolescent sociology, where everyone is watching their back and feels the need to keep up their emotional guard, midadolescents gather in friendship groups called *clusters*. We often confuse clusters with how we used to gather as friends in what most people call cliques. A clique, however, is a marker of late adolescence, where the bond between friends is so tight that members tend to exclude others from their group. A cluster is different. It is limited to midadolescence and is far more emotionally powerful than the cliques of late adolescence. As kids go underground to the world beneath, they instinctively grab onto a few others for protection—think *Lord of the Flies* and *Band of Brothers*. These friendship clusters are usually developed by tenth grade and exert power over their members throughout midadolescence. In some ways clusters vie for loyalty with the family, and with some issues the cluster's collective values will win out over the training and history of the individual kid's parents. They are based on bonds of mutual necessity and protection, but to your child they *feel* like the most intimate and sacred of families.

To be a student of your child means to get to know the people who influence him or her and get to know them well. That includes teachers, coaches, youth group leaders, and other parents, especially the parents of the kids in your child's cluster. Most of all, become a supportive and engaged friend of your kid's friends. Many parents think that their son or daughter wants them to disengage and back off from their world, but we have seen just the opposite, *so long as the parent does not invade their world.* To use a familiar image, your role is to sit on the steps of their world, get to know their friends, and celebrate the good that you find there while empathizing and having compassion on what is tough or ragged.

Maintain a Commitment to Dialogue

As you have sought to do throughout your child's life, make sure that the lines of healthy and warm communication remain open. It is *your* responsibility, *not* your child's responsibility. Your default position, especially if you have done a decent job of this in early adolescence, is to continue to expect, and if necessary gently but unapologetically demand, that you talk as often as you can about everything you can. In many cases it will look to parents as if their children do not want to be in dialogue and discussion, when in reality kids cannot stand feeling like they are being subjected to continual badgering and lecture. When we say "dialogue," we mean exactly that—two-way, respectful discussions that contribute to the trust and depth of the relationship in a way that ultimately builds up both the child and the parent.

Parents who are able to maintain this as a hallmark of their relationship with their child know that the most important thing they can do is to allow their kids into their own lives—their questions, their dreams, and their plans. Kids *want* to connect, but they need to be convinced that their parents want to connect with them. When you have a talk with your child, what is the content of the discussion? Does it tend to move into reminders of what they're not doing, or what they need to accomplish, or something you want to point out to them? If this is the case, it is no wonder that your child doesn't want to be a part of these "discussions," because they aren't! Also beware of pushing your own struggles onto your kids, implying by how you talk to them that you need them to be your "best friend" or, worse, your personal therapist. This is simply another form of abandonment. Instead, listen to and talk with your child. This will build the foundation which will make you able to handle those tough issues that come along as they go through this phase of life.

Be the Adult

As you push back the fence boundaries you have erected for and with your child and give them more freedom and trust, you absolutely must carefully, regularly, and proactively monitor their ability to handle the growing responsibility they have been granted. We do not advocate being a sleuth, at least not in the normal course of parenting your child, but we do insist to parents that they do whatever they can to know who their child is and to stay abreast of the decisions they are making with their life. Some parents are so laissez-faire that they ignore letters from the school, never check homework, make no curfew, and hand their kid everything from free use of a credit card to Internet access in their bedroom. Only a very rare high school student can handle that level of responsibility, and the odds are great that the child will suffer, probably greatly, from this form of abandonment and neglect. On the other hand, some parents make it clear to their kid that they are going to be deeply involved in their life, and that usually translates into behaviors like constantly overchecking schoolwork, sitting in on youth ministry meetings, and going through text messages in the middle of the night. Such overly controlling parents can cause kids to go further underground, sometimes in highly secretive and even destructive ways.

So how does a parent find the balance? How do you know when and how to secretly check text messages or homework and still maintain the kind of trusting and encouraging parental role your kid needs? You must help your child to know that as the parent and adult, you are responsible for helping them develop independence, responsibility, and healthy autonomy. In doing so, grant the privacy and independence that they have shown themselves to be able to handle. When they do something that forces you to trust them less or to get more directly involved in their lives and choices, negotiate that and work with them to assess and decide on the next steps. Your child may not appreciate it or even agree if you decide you will need to check their homework before they do anything else at night, but it is your responsibility to set an objective timetable for further loosening restrictions. In other words, when your child is making the kinds of choices where you do need to step into their lives, then make sure that they know why and, as best as you can, what you feel you need to do about it.

Another issue that we have seen come up with parents is having a hard time finding the balance between being a friend and being a parent. Some say you cannot be both. We adamantly disagree. Jesus himself, whom the Bible calls Lord and King, called his disciples friends the night before he was crucified:

> You are my friends if you do what I command. I no longer call you servants, because a servant does not know his master's business. Instead, I have called you friends, for everything that I learned from my Father I have made known to you.
>
> John 15:14–15

If the ruler of all creation allows himself to call those who followed him friends while retaining his stature and authority, then what makes us think that we cannot maintain our *temporary* authority with our children? After all, our goal is to get them to the place where they are dependent on the heavenly Father as they walk interdependently with others in community, including us. In other words, our objective is that they will eventually be our peers. You *must* think in terms of lifelong friendship with your kids as a central goal of the parenting task.

That said, again, how do you maintain the balance?

We believe that is the wrong question, and therein lies the problem—it is a false dichotomy, and so there is nothing to balance. You are a parent who also is operating as a caring and committed friend. Sometimes friends say difficult things, and sometimes friends intervene on behalf of what is in the best interest of their friend. By virtue of the role we have as parents, we also have the responsibility, even mandate, to make sure our friends are well served, well cared for, and well developed. So it is fine and good to be your child's friend, provided that you never lose sight of the fact that your role with that friend is a role of authority, leadership, and careful boundarying.

Be Reasonable

One thing is no secret to your kids: you are fallible and flawed. That means you will fail them. You will say things you do not mean, and you will do things that are not smart. The final thing to keep in mind as you boundary, guide, and launch your child into adulthood is to be a reasonable and teachable adult. The best parents do not hide their failures and mistakes from their children. Rather, they are real, live models of healthy adulthood for their children. This means things like asking forgiveness when you've blown it, accepting responsibility for not listening to or even for hurting your child, and apologizing for the *impact* something you did or said had on your kid, even if your *intent* made sense. If you are too harsh with a decision, change it later and explain why. If you believe that your child deserves a fairly stiff consequence but while in dialogue you see that they "get it" and are sincerely aware of their behavior and committed to growth and change, then allow yourself to pray, hug, and pronounce, "That's it; let's move forward." In other words, be the adult, but be a *reasonable* adult.

Building the Scaffolding for a Lifelong Faith

As your child enters midadolescence, they now have the capacity for dealing with the abstract nature of faith. Yet at the same time, because they are right in the middle of their adolescent journey, they do not yet have a clear understanding of either who they are (identity) or what it means to make the kind of decisions that have lasting impact (autonomy). This in turn creates a double-edged sword when it comes to a growing, mature faith. First, their inherent egocentrism spills into the way they categorize and flesh out their faith. In other words, although the heart of the gospel is a call to die to self, a midadolescent has a very difficult time understanding this and an even harder time putting it into practice. Thus their faith becomes about them—their wants, their needs, and a way out of trouble when they are desperate. Researchers have referred to this as "Moralistic Therapeutic Deism," and this understanding of the gospel is the norm among even those teenagers who faithfully attend church in the United States.[2] With the developmentally limited and culturally reinforced view that God is in the business of making my life comfortable, it is hard to get today's midadolescents to give much attention to a God whose invitation requires self-sacrifice.

The second challenge is perhaps even more of an obstacle to maturity for this age group—since they have no real idea of who they are, they live through different selves in different social settings. The problem is not that they are inauthentic in any one place or with any one group of people; it is that because they have not yet discovered their core identity, they have no other choice. Consider identity as a candle that glows from within us. As adults and late adolescents, that candle is at the center of who we are. We may compartmentalize, or let others only see one side of us, but as an adult (or late adolescent) we still have a single core identity, or one candle. Because their identity is a few years from being settled, a midadolescent lives through a variety of selves, or multiple candles. What makes this so difficult for midadolescents, parents, and Christian youth workers is that the candle of church and faith that they live out of in religious settings, like church or Young Life, is a true and honest representation of who they are, but *only in that setting*. When they are with their cluster, they live out of a different core self, or candle, which in all likelihood does not reflect the same worldview, values, or commitments as the self at church or youth group.

Despite these two limiting qualifiers, however, a midadolescent has the ability to begin to grab hold of some of the deeper dimensions of faith. The growth they experience may be so incremental that we may not even see it and at times be highly inconsistent to the point that we may not trust it, but many midadolescent kids' faith is alive, is real, and impacts every aspect of their lives. In light of this, here are five faith-building strategies that can help move your child toward a growing faith even while wading through the mire of midadolescence.

First, encourage a personal ownership of their faith. Every child eventually needs to make the leap from mimicking their parents' faith to taking on their own. This is among the most difficult of roads for parents, because this is where we ultimately have to sit back and allow the process to unfold. As we've said, parenting is a marathon, not a sprint, yet watching your son or daughter truly wrestle with faith as they attempt to figure out how much they are able and want to own it for themselves is painful at best. Just as Jesus told Peter to watch his own life and not fret about John's life with God (see John 21:20–23), we too must let our kids know that the faith journey they are on is theirs to walk, and our commitment is to support them as best we can.

Second, do what you can to encourage them to ask hard questions of life and faith and to not be afraid to deeply analyze and explore what they have been taught their whole lives. Every person's faith, and faith journey, is unique. Your child may have been a model Sunday school kid in kindergarten, an enthusiastic leader in sixth grade, a "student leader" in ninth, and yet by the end of their junior year they may tell you, "I don't believe in that stuff anymore." It is possible and even likely that it is not *Jesus* or even *Christianity* they are rejecting but rather something as amorphous as "the church," which is to them a monolithic, heartless, faceless institution that does not care much about them. Crisis and struggle are a prerequisite of growth, so without pushing too hard, don't be afraid to allow and even encourage your child to seek the truth with honesty and openness.

Two things to keep in mind here: First, a "claim" or pronounce-
ment like "I don't believe that stuff anymore" is not necessarily
an ironclad, once-and-for-all decision. Part of adolescence is
testing everything, from the outlandish to the inane. Nearly every
parent will hear at one time or another, "You don't even *know*
me!" But within a week, a day, or even an hour, they will come
crawling into bed with you late at night, telling you all about
the teacher they don't know what to do with. Take your child
seriously, but do not let the shifting waves of their struggles
shock you into defensiveness or despair. The respect you show
your child is vitally important, and so is keeping your cool, even
when you feel personally attacked or challenged. Remember,
much of midadolescent life is testing what they think, believe,
feel, like, and trust.

Second, sooner or later your child, if they care at all about the
church and their faith, will come to see that the church is not
all it's cracked up to be—not even close. You know it, we know
it, and somewhere around fifteen years old, they begin to see it.
The church is a ragtag collection of flawed, broken, self-centered
people who are all too often control freaks over the most ridiculous of things. This awareness is even more pronounced when
a child hits midadolescence, because what they are used to and
what is standard fare and acceptable in their world is so easily
put down, judged, and dismissed in the church. Whether the issue
is baggy pants, a short skirt, wearing baseball hats, or drinking a
soda in the sanctuary, the norms of Christian culture and church
life are not the same rules that kids deal with on a daily basis.
Some may put up with what often appears to them as an organized "out to get us" assault on everyone young, but sooner or
later most will just write off the institutional church and call these
cultural issues that fragment and divide our communities what
they are: stupid, shallow non-issues. (What we find interesting
is that adolescents are equally as invested in their "side" of the
story, all the while blaming adults for their lack of understanding,
compassion, and "chill." But that is another book.)

As parents and other adults who are invested in helping our
children mature in their faith, a third role we can play is to *help*

them to invite Christ to each setting and "self" they operate in. When it comes to faith, parents typically deal with their children on the level of behavior—like dress, language, and attitude—instead of on the level of their heart. Authentic maturity is not something that starts with behavior but rather is something that flows from a person's internal commitment to trust Jesus in every area of their life. To give God's Spirit a foothold in your child's soul, the best strategy is to discuss and dialogue with them about Christ's desire to be a part of their lives.

This needs to be delicately applied, for using these words alone will elicit anything from a "deer in the headlights" response to an outright angry reaction. It is vital that you are careful to introduce the Lord organically and naturally into conversations. If you are dealing with a certain problem with a teacher, for example, bring up how God is a fan and is there to help them with the teacher. Pray together for both the teacher and the setting (but *only* do this after your kid is convinced you are their fan and not lobbying for the teacher). The same goes for friendships, dating and sex, alcohol and drugs, or whatever is on their immediate radar—do your best to prayerfully look for gentle and easy ways to make Jesus relevant in any of these areas of your child's life.

The fourth strategy is to *empower your child to put their faith into action.* Today's parents have been raised in a decidedly modern culture—toward the end of it, to be sure, but many of the tenets and trappings of "Christian modernity" maintain quite a hold on most Christian parents. What this means is that we were raised to believe that Christian nurture takes place by attending Sunday school, listening to youth talks, going to camp, and attending church. If faith is boring, the answer is to get active in youth group or sign up for camp, a concert, or another event. The goal of youth ministry in the 1980s and even through the early 2000s was to teach kids truth and then try and make them passionate for God, meaning we designed programming so as to elicit from them an emotional, affective response to the faith they were taught (and unfortunately, many still think this is the single magic key to adolescent "discipleship"). For those who struggle in making sense of faith, or in trusting God in a particular area, or even with belief that God exists, the antidote is to barrage with them snappy Christianese and bumper-sticker-like theological platitudes and to deliver a logical apologetic argument for why it is better to live as a "committed Christian." In other words, the idea was that if kids were only taught proper truth (which almost always meant being exposed to the *ideas* that *point to* the truth) and given the chance to be with other kids who were "fired up for Jesus," they couldn't help but follow Christ with passion and abandon.

What many churches and youth workers are beginning to recognize, however (and that films like *Saved!* have highlighted in sarcastic detail), is that a superficial, logical, and emotionally driven faith has very little impact on the life of contemporary midadolescents. They have been abandoned, are deeply wounded and know it, and have very little trust in anything that even remotely smells like it has a self-serving agenda. For lots of today's teenagers, youth ministry "by the numbers" represents one more superficial, disconnected, and uncaring adult agenda that is to be trusted only at arm's length.

What it takes to win the hearts and souls of hurt kids today is to strip away the fluff and excess of cultural faith and head back into the core of the gospel: giving ourselves away for the sake of others. Unfortunately, the Bible's words about sacrifice, consistent lifestyle, mercy, and love for the poor and the needy have been pushed into the background of our understanding of faith. The last three parables in Matthew's Gospel, for example—the parables of the ten virgins, the talents, and the sheep and the goats—center on one theme that summarizes Jesus's life and teaching. It is found in the comparison our Lord makes between those who truly love him and those who settle for knowing about him:

> The King will reply, "I tell you the truth, whatever you did for one of the least of these brothers of mine, you did for me. . . . Whatever you did not do for one of the least of these, you did not do for me." Then they will go away to eternal punishment, but the righteous to eternal life.

> Matthew 25:40, 45–46

The only hope our kids have to develop into mature, committed, and powerful followers of Jesus is to be reconnected with these more demanding and costly elements of the call to faith. Lastly, the most effective thing we can do to foster spiritual maturity in our children is to *integrate them into adult relationships in the body of Christ*. Because midadolescence developed due to our collective neglect and abandonment, we must undo its effects by bringing adults and kids together. Young people should be allowed and encouraged to participate in adult Sunday school and Bible study classes, go on men's and women's retreats, and serve on ministry and service teams with adults. The more your child feels that they are part of something bigger than themselves and that they are included in not only *a* family but *the* family of God, the more they will allow themselves to be drawn into a level of faith that will strengthen and lead them for the rest of their lives.

Faith-Building for Midadolescents

1. Encourage personal ownership of faith.
2. Promote questions and exploration of faith concepts.
3. Help them to invite Jesus to each "self."
4. Empower them to put their faith into action.
5. Integrate them into adult discipleship relationships.

11

Parenting through the Seasons
Late Adolescence, Emerging Adulthood

Parenting isn't about raising children who fit some external model of "good" children. Instead, parenting is, like faith itself, about the process of becoming—not only for the child but for the parent as well . . . indeed, parenting is about more than raising children. It is about investing in our hopes for the world. It is about joining in with our Creator in the ultimate act of re-creation. It is about pointing our children toward the work God has for them and giving them the resources to do it.

Carla Barnhill[1]

Our oldest son, Chap Jr., dropped out of college after his sophomore year to move to Kenya to live with and learn from a community of Masai followers of Christ. Eight months later, as he was preparing to come home, he asked for some extended time with us and especially with me (Chap). While living with his hosts, he had come to see that he needed to talk through some things with me as he entered the next stage of his life journey. Essentially, what he needed to work through was how his perception of our relationship had impacted him in a way that was keeping him from growing into the man he was called to be. God had done some powerful work in our son's life during that time away and was able to get through to Chap Jr. in ways he had never experienced before. As a result, we were going to have a one-on-one "chat" where he would have "a few things to tell me" (and Dee was invited to be a listening third party). During the weeks and days leading up to our time, my emotions were running high and were mixed. On the one hand, I couldn't wait to be with my son and to see firsthand how the Lord had touched him. On the other, I was scared about what he was going to say.

Three days of intense and in-depth walks and talks later, we had arrived at a place where we were all three ready for his late adolescence. Neither of us ever got mad, or even anything more than mildly defensive. In retrospect, roughly a third of what our son said was muddy and perhaps debatable, a significant percentage of his critique of me and how I had hurt him was on target, and of course in a few areas his perception was simply different than mine or even more about him than me. The first day was rough on us all, but by the middle of the second day we knew that this was a tremendous gift and opportunity. By the third day we were on a new level of understanding, appreciation, and partnership. His assessment of me and our relationship during his growing up years was sometimes hard to hear, but ultimately the content was not nearly as important as the process, and that process helped us to achieve a new relationship out of some fairly rough midadolescent waters. As a result, our boy was ready to take that last step in becoming a man.

This chapter wraps up the process of adolescence and offers a few thoughts on what it means to parent someone who in many ways is far beyond parental control or sometimes even influence. Late adolescence is the last stop on the developmental road to adulthood, and it is the season where your attitudes, actions, and reactions present opportunities to help your child take that final step as an adult. It is gloriously fun, occasionally frustrating, and tantalizingly slow, but it is also a constant reminder of

how God so often sees and deals with us as we attempt to keep
at bay our own adolescent tendencies. In this stage your child
is almost a man or a woman, and being there for them through
this period is an honor and joy that is equally as precious as any
of the other developmental stages you have been through.

Late Adolescence—Still Adolescent, or Emerging Adult?

One of the leading scholars in the field of adolescent development, Jeffrey J. Arnett, is campaigning to change the term
that people use to describe that transitionary time in life when
one is nearly finished with self-centered adolescence and ready
to move into adulthood, roughly during the early and into the
middle twenties. Arnett does recognize that, as we have argued,
the essence of what makes up an adolescent is rarely fully completed until the mid-to-late twenties for most young people. Yet
as a leading developmental scholar whose primary concern is
with how society thinks about and treats college-aged and older
twentysomethings, Arnett believes that as long as we continue
to refer to someone as an "adolescent," we may hold them back
from living up to their potential as young adults. The term he
favors for this stage of development, then, is *emerging adult*.

We believe that Arnett makes a valid point. As parents it is easy
to get used to pigeonholing and categorizing our kids to the point
where we fail to recognize the incremental baby steps of growth
that they are taking as they head toward the end of the tightrope.
Many parents, seeing attitudes and behaviors that *appear* similar
to their earlier years, deal with their twentysomething children as
if they were seventeen. Although we do agree with much of what
Jeffery Arnett advocates in order to serve our kids with the most
helpful support they can have, we do not think that his reasoning
is compelling enough that we should completely disassociate
this late stage from the rest of the adolescent process by calling
it emerging adulthood. Our view is that while there is danger
in holding a child back by labeling them or asking too little of
them, we also need to remember that they still need a careful

eye and touch as they move through this final transitional phase of their lives. Whatever we call this stage, we as adults have the responsibility to do whatever we can to help others along the way in as healthy and productive a manner as possible. For example, when your twenty-four-year-old daughter calls to say she is changing jobs for the third time in eighteen months, you may find yourself retrieving and then playing at high speed the "you need to be more responsible" tape that you recorded years ago. Or after a conversation with your twenty-six-year-old son in which he laments how he can barely afford to eat on his salary, you may feel "forced" to send him *another* check, along with a note that tells him how he needs to be more accountable as you have "had" to pay off his fifth parking ticket. You may even shoot off an email that starts, "Fine, I'll pay the parking ticket! But I want to know, here and now, when are you going to grow up and stop being an *adolescent?*"

Harboring an attitude that labels our kids according to how far they have to go is telepathic. They can instinctively feel it, and it almost always produces the opposite effect desired. And when the attitude comes out in flagrantly derogatory or inflammatory ways, like with a public comment or a harsh parental email, a late adolescent will continue to feel discouraged and disempowered. An employer, parent, friend, or even spouse may *believe* that they are being helpful when they point out the residue of delayed adolescence or they respond to failure or weakness. But the best way to help a late adolescent to take those last few steps off the tightrope is to help them believe that they are worthy and capable of becoming an adult. For this to occur they need all the support and encouragement that those around them can muster.

That is the heart of the challenge of parenting a late adolescent. As Arnett points out, they are really emerging adults. Yet, as most parents will attest, they still have behaviors and attitudes that are far more adolescent than adult. The parental shift that needs to take place is grounded in a belief that growth is happening and your child will soon become an incredible adult peer. As with the other two adolescent stages, although your child is nearly ready to enter adulthood, you need a new awareness and a fresh commitment to be the kind of parent your child needs during late adolescence.

Understanding and Showing Compassion

For parents, this last stage of the adolescent journey represents a significant shift. The essence of late adolescence is more about the launching of a young adult than the corralling of a confused and volatile adolescent. As we have mentioned, the timing of this stage is not set according to outside social influences, like early and middle adolescence are. At the same time, for many it can last easily as long as the other two stages, if not longer (see chart below).

Stage of adolescence	Begins	Ends
Early adolescence	11/12	14/15
Midadolescence	14/15	19/21
Late Adolescence	19/21	Mid 20s?

Like the end of midadolescence, your child's move from late adolescence into adulthood demonstrates the desire and willingness to settle into adult roles and relationships. They will have landed on a general and relatively centered awareness of who they are designed to be. They will gradually move to the place where their word and their trustworthiness matter to them, especially in relating to those they respect and care about. They will also look for others with whom to walk through life in the kind of community where they not only belong but also contribute and serve.

A late adolescent has grown to the point where they now can begin to see how the perspectives and needs of other people matter. As social creatures, we are designed to rely on one another, and we celebrate the fact that every person has gifts and talents to offer the community. The move from dependence as a child to independence as an adolescent, then, sets the stage for a willingness to live interdependently with others in community. A late adolescent intuitively knows that this is both their calling and their trajectory as they begin to embrace their own adulthood.

The final step into adulthood, however, is difficult for many of our young today. There are several theories about why this is, from economics to the popular belief that "everybody needs a master's degree to get anywhere in life." In our work with late adolescents, we have seen that there are as many reasons for this being a difficult transition as there are people. Some of the more obvious external factors cannot be lightly dismissed, like economic realities and the need for more sophisticated prerequisites for entry-level jobs. On the other hand, lots of people in their early twenties have crossed the threshold from adolescent to adult without a graduate degree or any substantial savings and are doing fine integrating as capable, productive, and generally fulfilled members of the adult community. But for every one we have seen who has gone this route early, we have seen fifteen to twenty who have not.

> It may seem counterintuitive to most adults, but the last thing you want to communicate—verbally or nonverbally—to a late adolescent is that *they are still an adolescent!*

How can a parent be prepared to help their child through this last phase of adolescence? Unlike early and middle adolescence, late adolescence is a unique and highly individual experience. During the earlier stages, peers are given a high level of power as a young person moves along the tightrope. In late adolescence, however, the child is moving further and further away from peers as they decide who they are and where they want to go with their life. By this stage of the game your child will have written much of their own story, and it is a story they do not completely understand. At the same time, especially as friendships shift, new associations are built, and new gifts and talents emerge, this is when they need you to hear—and at times weep, laugh, and sing along with—their story. Understanding and compassion at this point are more about being a resource to them where you responsibly should and are able to be, being a gentle and reassuring sounding board, and offering guidance when it is asked for. Sometimes you may find yourself feeling the need to give unsolicited advice, but even in this case, you will need to ask for permission first. Your role is to treat them like an adult whom you love and are there for and at the same time to keep an eye out so you do not inadvertently empower them to extend their adolescence longer than makes sense.

Boundarying, Charting the Course, and Launching Them into Maturity

In setting the direction for this last stage, we need to allow for the process to run its course. We must beware of trying to force adulthood on our kids and instead cherish the amazing and profound growth that occurs during these last few years of adolescence. Our best shot at making the most of this stage is to focus on the three roles of parenting that help launch our children into adulthood:

1. Treating our children like adults while training them and providing resources for them as adolescents
2. Being a committed friend who offers timely guidance
3. Naming who it is that they are becoming

As we have emphasized, the movement from middle to late adolescence is the shift, much like a light switch, from egocentric abstraction, where most of life is filtered through a self-centered protective screen, to a relationally aware abstract ability to recognize how they treat others affects how others see them (okay, maybe it's a dimmer, but it's still a light switch). This is one of the most significant changes in development that has occurred over the past thirty years, and yet few adults are aware of how dramatic a change it is. Most likely you never experienced what we now call midadolescence, or if you did, it was in the early emerging stages of it, and it may have impacted your life and choices for only a couple of years. As adults we have a hard time seeing our kids' lives as being all that different from when we were young, but this book has sought to remind you of how dangerous that perspective can be.

As a parent of someone moving from middle to late adolescence, you get to see and celebrate the signs of this shift: Out of nowhere you will receive a phone call asking how you are doing (without any self-centered hooks), or you will be invited to engage in a dialogue that is actually a two-way discussion, or you will get money back after giving them a couple of twenties for a movie and pizza.

Once you begin to see the signs, you will need to move even further away from holding the power cards in the relationship and more toward being a guide, friend, and coach. Your role during late adolescence is to be their friend, to be clear about what you can and cannot do for them, and to treat them like an adult as much as you can. As a follower of Christ you are promised hope, for he will not leave you orphaned or stand aloof as you love and lead your child. Because as you trust him your destination is assured, you do not need to feel the weight of your child's decisions on your shoulders, *especially during late adolescence*.

> A late adolescent needs to know that others see their emerging calling take shape and to hear them regularly name it, even when they don't yet quite see it themselves.

This is the stage where your child has to decide who they are going to be and how they are going to live. But you still have hope, a hope that says that God loves and knows your child far better than you do. This same God, who has asked you to be his hands and arms in embracing the child he has loaned you and who has taught you along the way how to find the ability to be gentle, protective, and empowering all at the same time, now says, "I've got him!" and "She is mine!" In Christ, the markers along the way are not nearly as large as they feel at the time. Keep in mind that the joy of life is found in the road itself and not in how much we accumulate or what we accomplish along the way. Late adolescence is the time to stand backstage clapping, cheering, and watching your child take on life. Breathe in these days and enjoy your son or daughter. As Proverbs 29:17 reminds us, "Train your child, and they will give you peace; they will bring delight to your soul."

Building the Scaffolding for a Lifelong Faith

As you seek to help your son or daughter learn what it means to experience a vibrant, deep faith in Jesus Christ, consider the following four areas.

First, treat them like a spiritual peer. As we mentioned in the chapter on midadolescence, through their growing up years, it is important for you to be training your child to eventually see you as a friend. As they get older, one of the greatest if not the greatest gift you can give your child is to invite them to join you on your faith journey. For so many parents, the faith journey is primarily if not exclusively focused on pouring into our own kids' lives. As important as this is, if the family is the only place we live out our call as followers of Christ, we rob our kids of the best the gospel has to offer them. We have been designed to dance and sing and serve and cry with Jesus as we follow him in his kingdom work. The greatest satisfaction any parent can know is to stand arm in arm with their child, serving together in the name of Jesus.

Second, provide resources for the experiences that will help guide them into a deeper compassion for others and the world. When it comes to their faith journey, late adolescence is not

> For so many parents, the faith journey is primarily if not exclusively focused on pouring into our own kids' lives. As important as this is, if the family is the only place we live out our call as followers of Christ, we rob our kids of the best the gospel has to offer them. We have been designed to dance and sing and serve and cry with Jesus as we follow him in his kingdom work. The greatest satisfaction any parent can know is to stand arm in arm with their child, serving together in the name of Jesus.

the time to pull in the purse strings and become overly worried about getting your child to "take responsibility for their own choices." In most other areas of life, teaching your late adolescent son or daughter to tithe, save, be responsible, budget, and live according to their means is an important aspect of parenting. But when it comes to helping them to fully grab onto their faith, this is the time to give them as many varied opportunities as possible. When else will they be able to travel and spend a few days to several weeks with believers from other parts of the world? When will they be able to take the time off to hold a child dying of starvation, or play soccer with an orphan at a Compassion International or World Vision mission site, or pray and worship with Kenyan warriors in a grass hut church? Once adult life kicks into high gear, these kinds of life-changing experiences become few and far between.

We are strong and vocal advocates of this principle. So much of Western Christianity has been reduced to a series of proper thoughts about God and playing around with new ways to express our personal faith. But followers of Jesus have known for centuries that real life is found on the road, in the fields, in a home. Ministry and service are *the* central reasons the church exists; they are not just nice things to do when life and time and money allow for it. Your child has a far, far better chance at seeing and embracing the authentic King of heaven and earth when they are taken out of the ordinary, comfortable, and "normal" life they have grown up in and are thrust into another part of the world that God created, loves, and is on the move to restore. By being a part of God's work in the world, your late adolescent child will be able to put together the still somewhat scattered pieces of their faith and life.

Opportunities for missions, service, travel to other parts of the country and world, and connecting with people who are in deep need and who are also in love with Jesus are important gifts to your child throughout childhood and adolescence. But it is in late adolescence that your son or daughter is able to connect the dots of faith and vocation in a way that will not only honor your family's faith commitments but fine-tune and focus their calling as well.

Third, watch for their calling to emerge, and name what you observe. As often as possible, reinforce what they themselves are hearing and seeing about who they are and how God has wired them. Listen to your child's dreams and passions. Watch for what flows naturally from them, and look for ways to give them the best chance to see themselves in different and stretching contexts.

Many parents are not sure about this for their child—mostly because they are not sure about this for themselves. The concept of "personal calling" is foreign to the majority of Christian communities, especially in the United States. If this is your struggle, an important growth strategy for you is to seek out others who will help guide you in a process of discovering how God has created you to serve in his kingdom. Every person has a role, a vital role, in God's design for redeeming human beings. As you embark on the journey to grab hold of your place, grab your child's hand and take them with you.

Lastly, invite them into an adult place in God's community alongside others who will embrace and affirm them in mutual partnership in the kingdom of God. As we have said from the very beginning of this book, the greatest challenge facing society today is the systemic abandonment of our young. The church is the one place, the one family, in all of society that can address and reverse the effects of this abandonment. The ultimate goal for you as a parent is not so much to foster and develop a "responsible and productive Christian adult," but rather to create the atmosphere and choir of support where your child will always know, no matter what road they travel, that they always have a home.

Faith-Building for Late Adolescents

1. Treat them like spiritual peers.
2. Provide resources for unique experiences that will guide them into a deeper compassion for others and the world.
3. Name the uniqueness of their calling as it emerges.
4. Build toward a mutual partnership in the kingdom of God.

12

Six Longings of Today's Adolescents

When I approach a child, he inspires in me two sentiments; tenderness for what he is, and respect for what he may become.

Louis Pasteur[1]

Raising a child in a world that continues to spin at increasing speed and with fewer connections and less relational support than ever is, in a word, challenging. Not only are we forced to deal with culture and life as a nonstop moving target, but we also have all been swept up into society's penchant for living life from the outside, where image and performance are all that seem to matter. Hiding, defending, and deflecting whatever may cause us to look or feel bad has become our collective national sport, and few of us escape this pull. In the midst of this craziness, most parents still train and expect their kids to live up to those attributes that are necessary to allow us to live together—things like loyalty, honesty, and integrity. This is the great rub of parenting in a postmodern, fragmented, and relativistic world: How do we bring up our children as whole and solid people when all around them the way to make it through life is by taking shortcuts? Where do we focus so as to stay the course in our role as parents?

During adolescence a child becomes more adept at manipulating her world, has learned the art of pretense, and in many cases has discovered that life is much easier when lies flow freely. Life around us is not the only thing that makes parenting difficult; it is also how the collective "we" have allowed our inconsistent and feeble attention toward our children to drag them into the thicket of superficial and insincere living. We are not saying that our kids should not be held accountable when they lie, or cheat, or cut corners. We are not even saying that these and similar behaviors are not ultimately their responsibility. What we do believe, however, is that the world we have handed them has created such an individualistic and self-serving society that it is hard for them to even glimpse an alternate way to go. Sure, kids are clearly responsible for selfish and destructive behavior, but we are responsible for creating an environment where they often feel they have no choice.

So the question before us now is, what do we do about it? Another way to ask this is, what is our best response to behavior and attitudes that get in the way of our being a gentle and supportive presence in our kids' lives? We peer into those places inside of them that motivate them and drive them. We respond to those inner longings that they don't even know but that have a powerful influence on why they do what they do.

The Language of Longings

Our calling as parents, especially when our child is acting out or being distant or belligerent, is to diagnose as clearly and as fully as we can the various factors that are contributing to their angst. We must slow down and deeply listen to what they are saying, and not just with their words or facial expressions. The

Scriptures do not tell kids to avoid exasperating their parents, but rather the parents, specifically fathers, are told to make sure that level heads prevail in parent-child interactions (see Eph. 6:4). It is up to us to look behind their rhetoric, calloused looks, and sometimes defiant or occasionally confident attitudes and learn how to listen to their hearts and souls, even when their actual words would tell us they want nothing to do with us.

To get at what is going on under the surface of their busyness, hyperbole, and persuasive arguments and be able to hear the subtext beneath the observable text, we here offer you a tool to show how easy it is for parents to miss the subtext beneath the text. The table on page 167 describes six internal longings that all midadolescents hold inside, both boys and girls. In the left column, *What they say*, is an example of how this longing may be typically expressed. The middle column, *What we hear*, is how parents often receive that verbal message from their childen. Neither of these is intended to be exhaustive or precise. For you and your child, other words, gestures, and expressions may have worn a groove in the regular styles of communication you have created over the years. But both of these are examples of how easily kids and parents can get into ruts and communication styles that keep them from hearing each other. Yours might be different, but with few exceptions you have your own ways of missing each other, and that is the point of these first two columns.

The column on the far right, *What they mean*, shows what is often the real feeling and struggle behind your child's words and what he or she does want you to know but for lots of reasons cannot come out and say. The model describes what midadolescents are craving, even while they maintain the façade of the world beneath. Remember, they do not want to be abandoned! They are feeling lost and alone—and they authentically want adults in their lives who care! But all too often, because they are midadolescents and therefore still see so much of life through their limited lenses of self-interest and protection (remember, they are guided by egocentric abstraction), they will say things *they think they mean but are actually deeper cries for help that they don't even recognize themselves!* Our problem? We believe their words instead of paying attention to their deeper sobbing, their fears, and the longings that become the primary motivator of their behavior!

As you go through this chart, try to figure out where you and your child get tripped up both in how you communicate and in how you push one another's buttons. Do an analysis of how your child expresses these six longings. For example, what are the most common ways he lets you know he isn't feeling very important? Then do your own homework, with humility and honesty, and reflect on how your buttons get pushed and why. (This is, by the way, a great chart to use in bringing others into your life to help you discover what you are so close to that you may not be able to see for yourself.) Ask yourself, what is it that gets in the way of aligning with Ephesians 6:4 and makes me respond to my child in ways that exasperate her and ultimately make things worse?

We are convinced that not all family arguments are a result of parents falling into negative patterns or causing a breakdown in communication. With egocentric abstraction and the adolescent process in general, you are bound to face times when doing the best thing possible at the time causes your child to feel misunderstood, betrayed, and even blindingly angry.

We are *also* convinced, however, that lots of times, even in the best of families, parents do make things worse by how they talk or act. Sometimes, in fact, your child may come into a conversation with you and in a few short minutes become furious. A parent may look over at their spouse with a "What just happened?" kind of look, clearly thrown off that the encounter went south so quickly, honestly believing that they did nothing to contribute to the conflict, when they actually caused it. (Again, sometimes this has nothing to do with the parent, but sometimes it does, and that's the point here.) That is what this chart is for—to give you the chance to step back and attempt to discipline yourself to be as consistent a force of love, loyalty, understanding, and compassion as you can be, even as you hold the boundaries and authority during the adolescent process.

What they say	What we hear	What they mean
"You don't *know* me."	I don't matter to her.	*I long to belong.*
"You never listen to me."	He doesn't want to listen to *me*.	*I long to be taken seriously.*
"I can do it!"	She doesn't need me.	*I long to matter.*
"I'm *fine*, okay?"	He wants to be left alone.	*I long for a safe place.*
"It's *my* life!"	She doesn't care what I think.	*I long to be uniquely me.*
"Nobody cares about me."	He doesn't care about anybody but himself (me included).	*I long to be wanted.*

Six Longings of Today's Adolescents

Let's break down each of the things we hear adolescents say—and what longings are behind the true meaning of their words.

"You Don't **Know Me**" vs. "I Long to Belong"

Most parents of a midadolescent will hear this, or something similar, during the high school years, especially with their girls: "You don't *know* me!" Usually this is in response to what they perceive as a parent trying to put them in a box or stating something about them that they either don't like or are not even sure of themselves. What we too often hear in this kind of statement is that they want to push us away, that they don't care what we think or what we believe about them. We think, "I don't matter to her." The problem with this parental reaction is that it produces exactly the opposite of what your child actually needs. As a general rule of thumb, we as parents have got to work overtime to make sure that we don't allow ourselves to get swept up in the verbal sparring that is so much a part of both high school life and too many families. When we let ourselves get wounded by our kids' outbursts, global statements, or accusations—or worse, when we treat them differently or pout as a result of what they say or how they act—we drive them away from us. What parents need to recognize is that a midadolescent does not have the energy, or in some cases the ability, to work through what they are feeling and also have to worry about our emotional reaction to them.

In this case, when your child says something like "You don't even know me," remember, it is not about *you*. They are using you as a punching bag for their own inner struggle to connect with others. They have an intense longing to belong, and throughout midadolescence this is always a difficult longing because relationships feel so tenuous and unpredictable. So, parent, your job is to take it on the chin, curb your reaction, and do your best to acknowledge that your child is trying to figure out where they belong. Above all, do *not* become the learned amateur psychologist and tell them what they feel: "I get it—you long to belong, just like that great book I'm reading said!" No, that is a strategy that will surely backfire. Instead, here are four ways to respond when you sense that they have a need to belong:

1. Acknowledge that you care about them.
2. Let them know that it sounds to you like they may have some deep feelings going on that you may have triggered.
3. Let them know you want to know more about why they feel the way they do.
4. Let them know you'd love to sit and talk with them when they are ready.

"You Never Listen to Me" vs. "I Long to Be Taken Seriously"

As with the first statement parents hear, this one will have several variations, most often nonverbal. Most common are rolling eyes, folded arms, and a look of boredom or exasperation that screams out impatience with you, especially when you are in what they see as "lecture mode." When we sense this attitude, our typical response is to add even more force to whatever we are saying to make sure that we "get it through their thick skull!" We get mad because we don't think they want to hear from us and we think they don't respect our opinion or couldn't care less about what we have to say. Yet what they *say* is that we never listen to them.

In this case, the feeling of exasperation is understandable, at least from your child's perspective. This conflict highlights one of the classic communication problems that plagues parents and teenagers: parents complain that their kids don't want to listen to them, and kids say exactly the same thing about parents! When your child expresses, either in words or with an attitude, or even with body language, that they want to talk, without question your best default reaction needs to be to let them talk, uninterrupted. At times this may not be possible, for instance in public or when time constraints force you to come to some sort of resolution. For the sake of your relationship, however, and what is ultimately best for your child, you need to make sure that they *believe* that you care enough about them to hear them out, even when what they have to say may not be what you want to hear. The alternative is much, much worse.

An often ignored but universal truth of life is that the most intimate human activity anyone can engage in is *not* sex but conversation. Having an authentic, two-way, respectful, and honoring dialogue is the greatest gift any two people can give each other. Unfortunately, too many times parents get hoodwinked into believing it is their job to get information "through" to their kid. As a two-way conversation is a gift, this kind of attitude or behavior is about as big an insult as we can throw at someone. Your child deserves and desperately needs the gift of give-and-take talk. By disciplining yourself to slow down your instruction, wisdom, or agenda and learn how to truly listen to your child, you will communicate volumes more than you ever could with words alone. In that simple act of generosity, you are telling your child that what they have to say matters every bit as much to you as what you have to say to them. It tells them you are committed to taking them seriously. You may believe that you already take your child seriously and that they know it, but in how intently you listen to them, you prove whether that is true.

"I Can Do It!" vs. *"I Long to Matter"*

Adolescence is hard on everybody in a family. To move from childhood compliance through the struggle to become a unique individual, your child has to learn how to become independent. Because parents have, or *believe* we have, the wisdom that comes from experience, we have difficulty letting our kids make the mistakes that we are certain will lead to failure. Even the best parents have a hard time knowing when to allow developing independence to run its course and when to step in. This will always be a bit dicey, and you will make many mistakes over the years. Yet if you recognize that the place your child's defensive stance comes from has more to do with the longing to matter, in the long run you will have a much better chance at being received by your child as someone who truly cares.

During trying interactions with your kid, you may find yourself feeling like your child wants you to know in no uncertain terms that they do not need you. In the heat of the moment, they will inevitably remind you what a lousy parent you are and how if you would do what so-and-so's parents do (insert the name of your child's friend or a kid they sit near in geometry class), *then* you might *begin* to approach parenting mediocrity. During every phase of adolescence, your child will say hurtful things to you and accuse you of all manner of indiscretions. Some you will deserve, and many you will not. This comes with the territory of being an involved, committed parent. Making sure that you are doing all you can to help your child to know they matter is your chief concern during these years.

Unfortunately, lots of parents take so much control of their child's life that many kids do not have much chance to discover their unique identity, develop their autonomy, or even explore their calling and giftedness. When a parent is overly controlling, even with a young child, the kid can all too easily feel like they don't matter. And some parents go in the opposite direction. They treat their adolescent like an adult, even while she is desperate to rely on the fact that *you* are the adult. As she spreads her wings and makes decisions, you need to assure her that you are there for her, to listen, guide, and, yes, boundary. This is one of those vital dances of parenting—when we overcontrol, we participate in the larger avalanche of systemic abandonment toward our child, and when we undercontrol, we do the same. We must consistently work to offer balance to our kids.

"*I'm* **Fine**, *Okay?*" vs. "*I Long for a Safe Place*"

One of the more confusing things for parents of adolescents is how their child's emotions, temperament, and even personality can go through such wild swings. The stereotypical view is that this is reserved for girls, and what parent of a fifteen-year-old girl would not argue that even the metaphor of a roller coaster doesn't do the process justice? Yet when we go through the different moods and seasons where our child's personality bounces back and forth between two opposite poles, or when we encounter an unexplainable defensiveness or emotional retreat, we have to remember that for *both* boys and girls, the adolescent journey affects how they see themselves and how they behave.

The phenomenon is not only about chemical changes, as many flippantly assert. Rather, the complex convergence of multiple layers of confusion and insecurities swirling around inside the soul of an adolescent causes them to be significantly thrown off. Of course mood swings can be triggered by newly experienced chemical reactions, usually called "hormones," or even more serious chemical imbalances that need medical supervision and oversight. However, the parent who gets swept up in reducing the cauldron of adolescent moodiness and emotions to mere biology, *especially to or even in front of their child*, will not only misread them badly but will also cause them to flee as far from the parent as possible. The depth of confusion that adolescents feel on a fairly regular basis, especially from thirteen to about seventeen years old, causes them to react in ways that adults cannot hope to fully understand.

When our kid retreats or says or does something to communicate that they are doing just fine without us, what we hear and feel is that they want to be left alone. Often that is exactly what they *think* they want too. Occasionally your child may truly want you to get away and give them space. Again, as parents we tend to overreact by giving in to one of two extreme reactions. Either we take them at their word and give them all the space they say they need, or we push back and force them to stay engaged with us. The first reaction, granting them their expressed desire to stay away as long as it takes for them to come out of their room or their "funk," can be construed by the child as one more rejection, causing them to feel even more isolated and reinforcing the impression that nobody really cares about them.

The second extreme response, ignoring their implied (or even explicit) demand to let them find their way or be left alone, can often be viewed as discounting or even rejecting their need for independence and the freedom to work things through on their own, at least for a time. When we push too hard or demand that they work things through with us when they express the need for some time or space, they can feel like we do not respect them. By badgering or manipulating them to stay engaged, we can cause them to fall into a deeper sense of despair, for the added pressure is the last thing they want or need.

As parents we so badly want to help our child deal with whatever gets in the way of a happy life. That means our default reaction to any discomfort, any emotional outburst, or any number of uncomfortable to difficult situations is to try and fix whatever we see or hear—taken at face value. But we must remember that with an adolescent, a much deeper river of influence and motivation is always just beneath the surface of any issue they face. They carry inside of themselves deep and driving longings that are at the core of everything they say, think, or do. It takes so much gentle care and focused energy for a parent to sift through words and attitudes to get at the deeper feelings, insecurities, and longings that drive their child. Yet when we do take the time to look beneath the surface and to respect them enough to sit on the steps of their world, we put ourselves into a position where we can truly make a difference.

Once we do achieve enough trust for our child to invite us to see just a glimmer of what they face every day, what we discover can seem anything from counterintuitive to flat-out contradictory. Take this scenario, for example: When your son or daughter lashes out with words or an attitude that screams, "I'm fine, okay? Butt out, already! I don't need you!" it is hard to imagine that what they are really communicating is the longing for a safe place. Yet do not forget, defensiveness always comes from somewhere. When they push against you, often they are actually trying to say to you, "Don't you get it? I am confused, lonely, and insecure. I don't feel like anybody understands me or wants to. And when you push, or criticize, or even counsel me with sage advice, I feel *more* threatened and *less* understood. I long for a safe place."

If there is one single longing that summarizes this list, it is that. "Please," your child cries out daily, "someone provide me with sanctuary, with a shelter from the storm."

When they are feeling this way and their defensiveness or silence gives you a clue to their sense of aloneness, the task for you becomes obvious—to be that safe place for your child. Your presence, stability, sensitivity, and even timing can be the salve that is exactly what your son or daughter needs when they are at their most vulnerable.

"It's My Life" vs. "I Long to Be Uniquely Me"

As we've seen, at the heart of adolescence is the need to discover one's own sense of uniqueness. As society becomes increasingly fragmented and superficial, the support systems and structures that your son or daughter needs in order to do this are becoming scarcer and scarcer. By the time kids hit midadolescence, they become aware that they are on their own in the middle of this scary and lengthy trek. At the same time, they know that in order to make it in the world, they have to become *someone*. This tension—the feeling of being set adrift and isolated from everyone else competing with the need to keep moving forward in figuring out how to interact with a world perceived as uncaring and even hostile—fights against any authentic self-discovery process. Your child knows they need to grow up, and yet they feel that everything about the process is set up to make them fail. The greatest tension between parents and teenagers comes down to this inner struggle.

Objectively, we think it rather odd that a parent would chafe against a kid saying, "Hey, it's my life, not yours." That is, it seems strange until we realize that our emotions and reactions are so loaded with history and subtexts that we, like all parents, get distracted by the message even while trying to listen to the longing beneath the text. The deeper longing expressed by this attitude, however, is one that gets to the core of our kid's daily journey. When you hear, or even feel, your child communicate that it is their life they are dealing with, the only choice they make available to you is to stand beside them and let them know that, yes, it is their life, and you know it. Again, as we have said throughout this book, timing is crucial and so are facial expressions, genuine care and compassion, and any other tool in your kit that assures them of your committed belief in them.

Sometimes, especially when there is a bit of push and pull going on either in a discussion or over a period of time, you may hear it said like this: "It's my life, and *you can't tell me what to do*." (This one can easily be followed up by the proverbial, "And when I'm eighteen, I'm outta here!" to which we respond, destroying years of delicate parental pruning, "Yeah, and I'll help you pack!") We *think* what they are saying to us is that we have nothing left to offer them, or worse, that they don't care what we think. When we encounter a spirit or attitude that seems to say they don't want or need our input in their lives, the worst thing we can do is to take what they say personally, try to defend ourselves, or somehow communicate that we don't believe in them or they don't have the ability to make it on their own.

What your child is saying is, "I need to be uniquely me, and I feel like nobody's helping me to become myself. And I don't even know who this 'me' is." So when they come at us attacking or defensive or guarded in what they say or how they treat us, what they really mean is, "I am so alone in trying to figure out who I am; *please* don't get in my way. My life's hard enough without having to worry about pleasing you." What happens is that our kids so quickly interpret our attempts to care for them or to even engage them as a way to manipulate them and force them into our agendas and boxes (even if those are things they ultimately *need*). The longing your son or daughter feels is unique, and that means they yearn to be recognized as a person who has something to offer the world that only they can bring.

"Nobody Cares about Me" vs. "I Long to Be Wanted"

When you hear or even sense that your child is feeling like no one cares, what they are doing is offering you a gift: he or she being vulnerable and letting you into the pain of their personal world. This gift needs to be handled with kid gloves, gently caressing the wounds beneath the words and embracing the feelings behind the despair. On paper, this is almost obvious, and most of us can safely say we are already committed to responding with grace and mercy when our child lets us know how they are doing. But in real life, unfortunately, we get swept up in attitudes that can easily slam the door on the exposed raw places we have been offered. For many, our initial response may be to turn this around as being just one more expression of egocentric abstraction and to feel like our child needs to get over it.

We all know the expression "pity party." It needs no definition or explanation, really, for we all know it when we see it, and few of us have a hard time naming it when it pops up. Nobody likes whiners or complainers. "Life is hard—get over it," we say. "You're such a baby!" Granted, excessive complaining or nonstop whining needs to be dealt with when it is used as a tool for self-indulgence or to somehow manipulate the response of others. Especially during midadolescence, when the very essence of the stage is marked by self-interest and self-protection, we can find it hard to drum up too much sympathy when our child wants attention. As parents, however, we need to discern when we are getting played and when we are being allowed into that tender part of our child's soul where they are scared or sad. Yes, as parents we must deal with manipulation, but it is vital that we are careful to be sure that is what is happening. Sometimes repeated self-loathing or self-deprecating messages and behaviors may be *both* manipulative *and* at the same time an unveiling of a deeper pain. We believe that this is true in almost every case.

When we hear or sense that "nobody cares about me," it is amazing how quickly we want to turn that vulnerability around and use it to get sympathy for ourselves as parents. Out of our own hidden brokenness or insecurity, we can so easily flip the message and interpret our kids' whining as saying that they don't care about us. To ignore or explain away a statement or attitude where our child is feeling sorry for themselves can be devastating for them because what they actually want you to know is that they need to be reminded that you do care. Each of us, somewhere deep inside, wants and needs to be told that we are lovable, valuable, and cherished. Your child, even though they may not even be aware of it, carries around inside of them messages that criticize and question their worth. What they need, several times a day, are words and acts that consistently and without qualification proclaim their worth and value. What they are saying to you as a parent is, "I need you to *want* me—not because I'm a good football player, or I'm attractive, or you feel safe with me, or I'm dumb, or I'm loud, or I'm obnoxious . . . but because *I'm me*. And I wonder if *anybody* really wants me!" They are telling you that they may feel *loved* and even appreciated, but they long for a deeper, more sure word than that; they want to be *wanted*.

Believing you are wanted is similar to believing you are chosen, but it is even more profound. To know you are wanted not for how you look or what you accomplish or for how you do in school or on the field, but because you know you cannot survive without having someone in your life who says, "I choose you; I want you!" That's the longing your child carries through each day of the adolescent journey, and they want to know and hear they are wanted from *you*.

Being a parent means making sure we are the one who stands up by holding fast to our role and responsibility of being the adult. As you know all too well, words can wound deeply and sometimes take years to heal. Our kids hurt us, sometimes by the things they say and often by the things they do. That is part of the parenting experience as we love and lead a hurt generation. We must remember that our children do not mean to wound us. It can help to keep in mind that our kids are far too consumed with trying to become, or rather discover, who they are to proactively scheme to lash out at someone else. When there is pain and conflict, almost always they didn't mean it personally; we just got in the way.

Our role and calling is to be the adult. Our job is to listen and look as deeply as we can to what is behind their words and underneath their behavior. Discipline, nurture, and training require that we work hard to show compassion and to understand what adolescents feel, experience, and mean. That's all we really have to offer our kids when they are feeling lost, or stuck, or even desperate. But that's okay, because that's what they are longing for: love.

13

Parenting as Partnership
The Three Levels of Partnership

*Why do we keep hiding our deepest feelings from each other? We
suffer much, but we also have great gifts of healing for each other.
By hiding our pain, we also hide our ability to heal.... We are called
to confess to each other and to forgive each other, and thus discover the abundant mercy of God. But at the same time, we are so
terribly afraid that we may be wounded even more deeply. This fear
keeps us prisoners, even when the prison has no walls! How radical
Jesus' message of love is! How difficult! And how necessary!*

Henri Nouwen, *Primacy of the Heart*[1]

Now you are the body of Christ, and each one of you is a part of it.

1 Corinthians 12:27

One of the fundamental guiding principles of our culture is the
claim that how I live my life is solely up to me. It is my business
and no one else's.

This view takes many forms. Whether it comes when someone offers us unsolicited advice or in that nagging internal voice that lets us have it whenever we feel like we may need help, we have been taught since our earliest days that it is right and good that we take care of (or "mind") "our own business." To be an adult we must strive for complete self-sufficiency. Not only that, but most of the time we tend to like it that way. When it comes to making plans, creating strategies, or deciding a specific course of action for just about anything we face, we have been well trained to operate as if we are completely on our own. As Nike once told us, *Just do it!*

Unfortunately, while this cultural value we have bought into may help us to avoid being judged, evaluated, or critiqued, it also brings with it a destructive power for which we are all paying dearly. Somewhere deep inside we all know better than to believe the message that we are better off alone, but the pull is so ingrained that we do not think we are able to do much about it. The theme song of *Cheers*—"You want to go where everybody knows your name"—says it well; it is obvious how badly we really do want others in our lives. Yet we continue to build our fences and walls to keep others at bay. We are busier than ever and have every techno-gadget at our disposal, yet we feel sad when we slow down enough to wonder why nobody called. We want to be left alone, and at the same time we want someone just to sit with us. We are desperate for connection, but we hate the thought of someone actually connecting to us! We know we need advice, but we are reluctant to receive it. We recognize the value of an outside and unencumbered perspective, but we reject distant hyperbole and neatly packaged platitudes.

We are hungry for consistent support and encouragement, yet we also know that we can have it only when we get desperate. We know that deep, intimate, trusting friendships take time, energy, and no small amount of risk. We want others in our lives but can't stand the thought of being rejected after putting ourselves on the line. So we carry on, living as if we don't *really* need anyone, hiding our isolation and sadness even from ourselves.

This is where we have come as a society—we know we need others, we even *want* others in our lives (at least in theory), but to unravel our deeper commitment to privacy and to make sure we look like we are on top of our lives is a tall order. We need a radical transformation and a brand-new outlook on what it means to live in community. We really have no choice, not only for ourselves but also in order to be the parent that our child needs and we are called to be. For some this is the most difficult part of parenting—letting others into the journey. But in parenting the stakes are so high and the tasks so daunting that we have to do whatever it takes to get over our default need to look like we know exactly what we are doing. We have to let others in.

Yet it remains hard. Nowhere is this dilemma more pronounced than when it comes to our family. We want to be better parents, but for lots of reasons we are hesitant, and sometimes downright unwilling, to let others into our parenting. We find it hard to trust others' viewpoints and philosophies (with the occasional exception of a distant authority, like, say, an author or radio "parenting expert"). To suggest that we need or even want help is one of the central comedic themes of our society. In television shows like *7th Heaven* and *Everybody Loves Raymond*, we are told how we are supposed to live. The prototypical mother-in-law of *Raymond* highlights the downside of the pushy outsider on the one hand, and the "we have what it takes to figure it out ourselves in just under an hour" marriage and parenting of the Camdens on the other keeps the rest of us from letting anybody into the secret side of our parenting issues and struggles. No wonder we are afraid to let others in—in our culture we have so few models that offer a different perspective.

Inviting Others In

Although it has been drilled into us that our opinion is the only one that matters, God has not designed us to live that way. We have so much to learn from each other and so much to give. From the very beginning we were created to walk together through life, and we are only able to approach the fullness of what it means to live when we are in intimate, honest, and open relationships with others. What at first may seem hard or even frightening, and definitely countercultural, is actually quite the opposite. Community is how you were created to live, and therefore it is how you were designed to parent. But we need to be convinced that it is worth the effort and that it is therefore far better to include and walk with others as you lead and love your child than to hide behind a façade of health and wholeness.

If honest, most parents do recognize the need to open their lives up to others and invite them into the inner circle of their parenting and family life, but they are simply afraid. We can sing about community at church or even nod when it comes up in a Bible study or small group, but to actually try to live it is quite another thing. As well-trained isolationists, at our core we are skeptical of real, honest community; it feels so radical and naïve. To consider that life together is an essential aspect of God's design for us is threatening at best. It is so hard for us to believe that there is a better way to live.

At the same time, we like some things about holding our own reins and being in total control of our own little fiefdoms, like never having to admit a mistake or being forced to acknowledge our inadequacies. Yet the dark side of our commitment to living disconnected from others is that we then have nowhere to go when we find ourselves face-to-face with our own vulnerability. A seventy-year-old man whom we consider a friend once said to us, "Men don't have friends; they have acquaintances and competitors. I have no friends." But he *did* have friends—us—and *he needs us*, and lots of others, to be his friends. We all need friends who love us, listen to us, and are there to embrace us even when we are wrong or pig-headed or we fail. When we go at life alone, trying to live up to the cultural ideal of self-sufficient independence, we have nowhere to turn with our brokenness, insecurities, and loneliness.

Every parent will face days on the journey filled with deep sorrow and profound emptiness, and maybe even paralyzing fear. Perhaps the biggest issue we will ever face as we lead and love our kids is our own reluctance to have our truth exposed and our darkness and fear laid bare. We wonder, especially in the darker moments, if someone were to see the struggles and the warts beneath our carefully crafted veneer of health and happiness, would we be criticized, labeled, or cast aside? We are not sure whom we can trust with our kids or even with how we parent. We look around us and see all those other marriages and families who have figured it out, who are doing great, and who are collecting bumper stickers that tell the world that their kid is the superstar of his middle school, and we instinctively know that we had better buck up and fight for first prize in the Great American Parental Olympics. So on we run, hoping that we can all survive the process of raising our kids alone.

> We may yearn for friends whom we can lean on and learn from, we may cry out for models and mentors, and we may crave a safe harbor for our family but feel the challenge is beyond us. *But it is not!* This kind of open, exposed, and risky life together is what we have been created and designed to experience. Community is there for the taking; we just need to trust it, start slowly with a few friends we trust, and build from there.

How can we step off this treadmill? Is it even possible to find others who are able *and* who are willing to enter into genuine community without judging or dismissing us? At the deepest level we wonder if we will be able to find the courage to be vulnerable and real with something as sensitive as our kids.

Finding people we can learn to trust is a very real concern for most of us. In a society that values the result more than the process and the externals more than the heart, finding others who have the courage and willingness to embrace the messiness of real life relationships seems too great a task on top of everything else we have to worry about. Most of the people we know do not even try to pursue this level of community, usually because they do not think it is even possible in today's rapid-fire, prop-it-up culture. We may yearn for friends whom we can lean on and learn from, we may cry out for models and mentors, and we may crave a safe harbor for our family but feel the challenge is beyond us. *But it is not!* This kind of open, exposed, and risky life together is what we have been created and designed to experience. Community is there for the taking; we just need to trust it, start slowly with a few friends we trust, and build from there.

Entering community is not just a good idea for you as a parent; it is the very best way to reverse the pressure of abandonment for your child. We all need and are hungry for relationships that matter and for friends who will be there for us. When it comes to our children, however, they need to know that they have people out there whom they can count on to be there for them. They need models and fans, not only in life but especially as they make the shift from mimicking your faith to claiming it for themselves. We all need community in order to be whole and to grow. Your child needs you to be in community so that you have access to the vast resources of God's family as you make decisions in how you lead and love your child. And your child needs community because Jesus has declared that community is what it takes and means to follow him.

How we have worked this out in our own lives is by viewing life as a series of intimate, connected relationships. As we give more weight to those relationships that are clearly primary, like our walk with Jesus and our marriage, we put them at the center of our lives and live from there. The following Circles of Relationship model has helped us over the years as followers of Christ, marriage partners, parents, and friends.

The Circles of Relationship: A Model of Boundaries, Priorities, and Living in Community

Most people struggle to put into practice God's call to develop an intimate and honoring marriage, to be proactive and caring parents, to live in intimate community with others, and on top of all that, to have a life. When we got married, we were taught that we needed to make a concerted effort to "live by priorities," meaning to make sure we are giving enough attention to those things and people that matter the most. For several years we listened to others and tried our best to do this, for we have always known how important it is to stay focused on what matters. We also know that priorities are biblical. When Jesus said, for example, "Anyone who comes to me must hate his wife" (see Luke 14:26), he meant we must maintain our relationship with him as the highest priority in our lives, and everything else is secondary to that.

Living by priorities is vital, especially when we have so many different agendas pulling at us. Where most of us get tripped up is when we try to put this into practice. What does it *mean* to live by priorities? We typically start by making a list of what is most important in life, something like this:

- God
- family
- job
- church
- life

But for us, and we think for most people, this type of linear priority checklist is not very helpful and may actually be negative as we try to faithfully follow Jesus, love our spouses, parent our kids, stay involved at church, and eventually, if we have time, live our lives. Obviously each area is important and needs attention, and the list rightly assumes we place each one in a hierarchy of value. The problem is, we tend to approach a list like this not by giving each arena its proper weight in our lives but rather by treating each like a plate to spin, with some plates bigger and more important than others. As we address each priority in its own unique category, our default tendency is to compartmentalize our lives as we frantically try to keep each plate spinning. The problem is that we cannot keep this up very long, and even when we can, we end up living disconnected lives, constantly worrying about the individual parts instead of experiencing the whole as God's free and gracious gift. As we keep this up, we end up sacrificing the reason we developed the list in the first place.

As the Bible teaches, giving attention to the things that matter (i.e., making God first, fulfilling the call of a God-joined marriage, caring for our children, living together as God's family) is important and even essential for the follower of Jesus. But trying to live according to a list of "good" priorities doesn't work for very many, and especially not for us. In response to this dilemma, several years ago we came up with the Circles of Relationship model that takes the list and pulls it together so that we can see life as a whole. By recognizing that the life God invites us to is lived from the inside out and that we are called to give our all as best we can wherever we find ourselves, this model gives us a picture of what that means and looks like. In this way we are able to live with God at the center of everything we are, say, and do. Flowing out from that relationship, we are able to love our spouse in a way that honors them and builds them up, and together we then can care for and nurture our children. Finally, we invite others to join the life journey with us as "soul mates" or intimate companions.

> Life from the Center is a life of unhurried peace and power. It is simple. It is serene. It is amazing. It is triumphant. It is radiant. It takes no time, but occupies all our time. And it makes our life programs new and overcoming. We need not get frantic. He is at the helm. And when our little day is done, we lie down quietly in peace, for all is well.
>
> —Thomas Kelly,
> *A Testament of Devotion*

Partnering Level #1—Trusting the Spirit

The message of Jesus can be summarized in one sentence: "Be reconciled to God" (2 Cor. 5:20). Everything the Bible says about faith flows from this central truth of the gospel. It is what was intended in creation, what was lost when humanity turned our backs on God, and what is being restored in and through those who belong to Jesus Christ. In creation and through the cross,

God has invited you into an intimate relationship with him at the center of your life. This is God's story for you—that because of Jesus, you have been set free to know, love, serve, trust, and follow him as his beloved child.

Trusting the Spirit

Circles of Relationship

What does this have to do with being a parent? *Everything!* For although this chapter is near the end of this book, your sincere, focused, and proactively submitting love for Jesus Christ is where your calling as a parent begins. *Seeing how his love works in action through you* is what convinces a child that they are safe, secure, valued, and cherished. That is what the Circles of Relationship model is about—learning what it means to follow Christ from the depths of who I am and then living out of that relationship by pouring into the others whom God has granted me.

To develop your "parenting community," you must first acknowledge that everything you have to offer not only your kids but every person you encounter flows out of this first love. The Spirit is there for us, guiding us and whispering encouragement, comfort, and love to the depth of our souls. "The Spirit helps us in our weakness," Paul tells us. "We do not know what we ought to pray for, but the Spirit himself intercedes for us with groans that words cannot express" (Rom. 8:26). And it is this same Spirit, the Spirit of Jesus, that gives us hope, "the hope of glory" (Col. 1:27). Partnering with the Spirit of God allows us to keep our focus on his agenda instead of ours. Selfish ambition is cast aside when we allow ourselves to be deeply immersed in the Spirit who lives within the follower of Jesus. All community that means anything comes out of an individual's commitment to living from the center.

Partnering Level #2—Partnering with Your Spouse

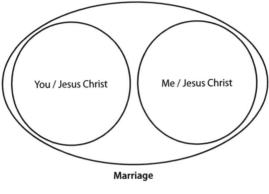

You / Jesus Christ   Me / Jesus Christ

Marriage

Circles of Relationship

The Bible tells us that in the beginning, it was "not good for the man to be alone," and therefore God created woman (Gen. 2:18). The woman, Eve, was created to be a complement to the man. She was his *ezer*, usually translated "helper" but closer to rescuer and partner than servant or assistant.[2] When God set up his world, he designed it so parents could work together as intimate and connected companions.[3] God's original blueprint in creation was to have children brought up within the safe and communal context of two parents, a man and a woman. In this most crucial of tasks, with two parents who first trust in God and out of that relationship rely on each other's unique temperament, giftedness, and even gender distinctiveness to care for a child as a *parental community*, the child is provided a much stronger base of support from which to explore life. Regardless of where your own theological tradition or background leads you in the specifics of this, the creation account makes it clear that in the grand scheme of God's design for the world, men and women need each other to live as partners, and never more than when it comes to parenting.

What about single parents? We are convinced that God recognizes, understands, and has compassion for the unique and additional challenges that come with being a single parent in today's world, especially when the other parent has abdicated their responsibility to love and nurture their child. Every issue and challenge we have talked about in this book gets magnified in a single-parent household, at least to some degree. But, while we do not for a minute want to risk diminishing the reality or even heartache of your circumstance, we do believe that at the same time a God-ordained extra measure of hope, strength, and encouragement is available for the single-parent family. God has proclaimed for both you and your child that he knows what you are going through and what you need, and he promises to hold you close.

As the self-proclaimed "father to the fatherless" (Ps. 68:5), our God is faithful, merciful, and kind toward you and your child. Regardless of the odyssey that has led you to where you are now, he wants you as a single parent to know with certainty that although others may desert you or you may feel helpless and alone, he will be an unwavering source of hope, power, and strength for you and your child. His character is fixed, and his heart goes out to those who have been wounded and who are in need, "For the Lord your God is God of gods and Lord of lords, the great God, mighty and awesome, who shows no partiality and accepts no bribes. He defends the cause of the fatherless and the widow, and loves the alien, giving him food and clothing" (Deut. 10:17–18).

For couples, this same promise and power is also what gives you hope in the journey of raising kids. God has not abandoned you to your own devices. Many of us, however, can allow ourselves to feel that way at times, as if Jesus were saying, "I have given you this child, now *don't mess up!*" Instead, his promise to be present and strong is what gives us the courage, wisdom, and insight to press on as we nurture our child in his name. At

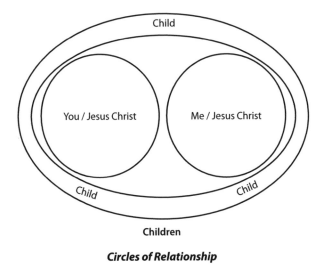

Circles of Relationship

the core of his plan for bringing up children is what happens when a couple does live their calling out in partnership. As a part of his consistent gift of mercy and grace, God's principal means of providing for you as parents is through the gift of each other. As you both trust in him and commit to partnering and supporting one another, you are provided another way of accessing the Spirit of Christ because of the Spirit's presence in each of you. This is what gives the marriage as parenting community its greatest punch—it is the Spirit in both partners that provides the counsel, wisdom, and insight we need to love our kids. This is the essence of God's design for parents: to work as partners in seeking God's best for your kids. That means listening to each other and listening *together* to God's Spirit as he works with and through you as you love your child.

Partnership Level #3—Inviting in a Few Soul Mates

As important as it is for your child that you as parents partner with the Spirit and with each other, in order to counteract the cultural abandonment our children have experienced, we

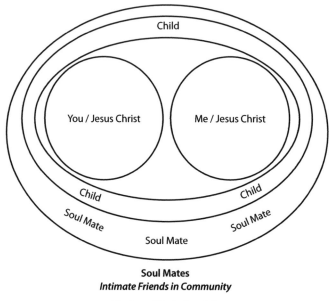

Soul Mates
Intimate Friends in Community
Circles of Relationship

need to offer them one more layer of consistent support: lifelong adult *soul mates*. As you cultivate an honest, rich trust in Jesus and love, listen to, and serve one another as partners, you are next called to draw around your family a community of close and trusted friends to include in your journey. Parents who are committed to maintaining a vital faith and have created a viable partnership do have the greatest influence on the lives of their children. But even in the best families, with the most respectful, balanced, and loving parents, our kids need more. Everywhere they turn today, kids are under the expectations and agendas of multiple adults and adult-run systems that seek to use, corral, and pigeonhole them. Parents help to soften this abandonment, but they need help. You and your child need a larger community of friends, and especially a few soul mates, to help guide, protect, and shape you as you journey together.

When we were first married, we were invited to help start a couples Bible study group with some close friends. Six couples came together and decided that we would attempt to go after life as a mini-community. Before long we began to recognize that if we really wanted to experience anything that mattered in the group, we would need to move beyond being a "reading circle" that only looked at and discussed the Bible as a doctrinal handbook. We knew we needed to talk about how God wanted to use the text *and each other* in helping us to grow and mature—in our jobs and careers, in our marriages, in our longings, and in our parenting. In this little group only one couple had kids, but in a few years most of us had started our families, and these were rich days. We supported each other, and we pushed each other. We laughed and got mad and advised and got defensive. When someone would start to pout or retreat, we would quickly rally around them to make sure that they knew we were in this together.

Six years later we were called to Colorado, and leaving our group was one of the most painful issues in the transition. Our kids belonged to them, and their kids belonged to us. Our plans, dreams, finances, and even different marriage and parenting convictions were issues we refused to hide from each other. Because of the intentional and yet organic and natural community God granted us, we not only came to value and even love being in community but also grew in powerful and unexpected ways during those years. We had indeed become family, and God changed us all.

Throughout our twenty-six-plus years of married and parenting life, we have sought out and been connected to similar groups everywhere we lived. Some were less formal, but each maintained the same sort of familial commitment and authenticity. Our last formal group, which only recently amicably parted ways, was our most intentional in making sure our relationships were rich and deep not only with each other but with each other's kids as well. For instance, when Ralph and Judy's daughter, Beth, was getting married, Ralph walked her down the aisle and Chap performed the wedding, but our group knew it was our little community of six families who were the sending and surrounding community that Beth (and her new husband, Matt) could count on. When Dave and Annie finalized their son Nathan's adoption, we were there in the courthouse for the celebration of the ages. Just as with our first group, we remain in many ways family. This is what community is all about—we belong to each other, even as we belong to Christ. And that belonging includes our kids.

To honor your trust in Jesus, to protect and deepen your marriage, and to help your child experience the best possible environment as they grow up, we believe it is important to live from the inside out. We believe that the Circles of Relationship model can help you to develop the kind of parenting community that every family needs and desires. In summary, this is what the Circles of Relationship model looks like:

1. **Each parent must seek to know, love, and follow Jesus Christ** from the center of their lives. The only way to provide a sense of wholeness and health is by inviting God into the central place in the family, and that invitation comes from within each parent who trusts in God.

2. **Both parents must be a cohesive and impenetrable unit of strength and love.** For those who are married, Jesus says that God has joined you together (see Matt. 19:6), and therefore your marriage is the most sacred and important human relationship you will ever have. So the best way to love and serve your child together is to build upon that foundation by providing a safe and stable home and functioning as partners. Kids have an amazing ability to divide and conquer as they try to take control of their own destiny. Each parent must be sure to help their children to understand and appreciate that your commitment as parents is to work together for the best of the child.

3. **The family must be surrounded by intimate friends in community, or *soul mates*.** To believe that they are truly surrounded by a supportive and caring community of "fans," your child needs to have at least a handful of adults who know their name, who pray for them, and who are committed to walking with them as individuals. A *soul mate* is not just a committed friend to one or both of the

parents but is committed to the entire family as a unit *and* promises to be long-term intimate friends with each child.

4. **Single-parent families need *soul mates*.** Single parents can easily feel that options for developing a parenting community are hard to find. Yet it is not only vital for you as a single parent to find a deep, rich community of intimate friends but essential for your child as well. While church-based small groups can commonly seem to slide into couples groups, ask your pastor or friends at church to help you find a small group or other community.

As you take care of your own need for intimate friendships, we suggest you do whatever you can to find some adults, both men and women, who will walk alongside you and your child over the years. This is what it means to be the church, and it is the best way you can partner with Jesus as he fulfills his promise to be a "father to the fatherless" (or "mother to the motherless") for your child.

In Conclusion

That kind of partnership—with the Spirit, with each other, and in community—is the best gift you can offer your child as you go through these years. Adolescence began because society was too busy and preoccupied to assimilate its young. Adolescence lengthened as adults abandoned the call to love and nurture their children into adulthood. Today's kids have been deeply wounded, and it is up to parents and the body of Christ to turn the tide of systemic abandonment. God's call is to do this by inviting our kids into the kind of community they were created to know and experience.

As you lead and love your child, know that the God of creation and the Lord of mercy goes before you.

Notes

Introduction

1. John Calvin in *Golden Booklet of the True Christian Life*, as quoted in Richard Foster, ed., *Devotional Classics: Selected Readings for Individuals and Groups* (San Francisco: HarperSanFrancisco, 1993), 167.

Chapter 1: Holding On for Dear Life

1. "The Mindset List" from Beloit College is released yearly. This list was accessed on November 27, 2006 at http://www.beloit.edu/~pubaff/releases/mindset_2008.htm.

Chapter 2: The Power of Love

1. The team we refer to is comprised of a group of Fuller Theological Seminary students and former students who have continued some of the initial work that I (Chap) did in the research for my book *Hurt: Inside the World of Today's Teenagers* (Grand Rapids: Baker Academic, 2004).

2. Patricia Hersch, *A Tribe Apart: A Journey into the Heart of American Adolescence* (New York: Ballantine, 1998), 19.

Chapter 4: The History and Meaning of Growing Up

1. Elizabeth Stone, quoted at Journeywoman.com, http://www.journeywoman.com/journeydoctor/travel_for_two.html (accessed July 14, 2006).

2. See for example Hans Seabold, *Adolescence: A Sociological/Psychological Analysis*, 4th ed. (New York: Prentice-Hall, 1992). The progression of adolescent development is well documented in psychological literature and is summarized in Chap Clark's book *Hurt: Inside the World of Today's Teenagers*.

3. *Metanarrative* is used in a variety of ways, but in this context it can refer to all those expressions of a culture that bind a people together. Originating from the combination of *meta*, meaning "grand" or "summative," with *narrative*, generally described as "story," this word is often used to describe the idea that every people group has a common story—expressed in narrative, literature, religion, song, and dance—that gives them a common history and corporate identity.

4. There is even a scholarly journal called *IDENTITY*, which describes itself as "the official journal of the Society for Research on Identity Formation."

5. Henri J. M. Nouwen, *Life of the Beloved* (New York: Crossroad, 1992), 45.

6. You can access a personal test called "Locus of Control" at http://www .psych.uncc.edu/pagoolka/LC.html. This test is based on J. B. Rotter (1966) "Generalized Expectancies for Internal Versus External Control of Reinforcement," *Psychological Monographs* 80 (1, Whole No. 609).

Chapter 5: The Changing Nature of Every Child's Journey into Adulthood

1. David Elkind, PhD, a professor at Tufts University, is considered by many the leading advocate of children in a culture of change; see his book *The Hurried Child*, 3rd ed. (New York: Perseus, 2001).

2. Some say that in the U.S. female puberty begins on average as young as eleven years old, while others say it is holding relatively steady at twelve. Regardless, this is much younger than a few decades ago.

3. By *macro* we mean that much of what we say in this book is for the broad stroke of young people, and that means there will be exceptions to everything we say. One important note on this, however: Even those adolescents who are not *directly* participating in behaviors reflected in this and other chapters have grown up in a world where they are clearly *exposed to* and a *part of* the macro world of adolescents. In short, our kids are not immune to destructive cultural forces.

Chapter 6: Systemic Abandonment: Or, How Did We Get Here?

1. David Elkind, *All Grown Up and No Place to Go: Teenagers in Crisis*, rev. ed. (New York: Perseus, 1998), 3.

2. "Pop Warner History," Pop Warner Little Scholars, 2005, http://www.pop-warner.com/history/pop.asp (accessed May 11, 2006).

3. Without a doubt, in many small towns across the U.S., student fans still turn out for major sporting events. But the interest in and enthusiasm for that supposedly enduring high school ritual has waned to the point that the event barely resembles the "school spirit" of the past.

4. Joseph Doty, "Sports Build Character?!" *Journal of College & Character* VII, no. 3 (April 2006), available online at http://www.collegevalues.org/pdfs/ Sports%20Build%20character.pdf (accessed June 2, 2006).

5. For a perfect example of how we now see sports as character building, even for children, see the syndicated article by Ray McNulty, "Politicians Forget That Sports Builds Character," available online at http://www.fox23news .com/sports/commentary/story.aspx?content_id=FFF78DB5-C6A1-4A6F-8BC3-

5D451A98B032 (accessed June 2, 2006). Although the author is referring to high school sports, his deeply reaching sarcasm seems to apply to even the youngest of sports participants. We would not completely disagree with the author if he were to stay focused on varsity high school athletics, but the article seems to offer a sweeping indictment of all who would caution against the "winners and losers" view of competition. If this is what he means to convey, we believe Mr. McNulty's viewpoint goes beyond offensive; it is dangerous.

6. "Cardinal Principles of Secondary Education," a report of the Commission on the Reorganization of Secondary Education, appointed by the National Education Association, United States Government Printing Office, Washington, DC, 1928, can be viewed online at http://tmh.floonet.net/articles/cardprin.html (accessed May 11, 2006).

7. http://www.wwe-club.com/phpBB2/viewtopic.php?t=54045 (accessed May 11, 2006).

Chapter 7: The Five Tasks of Parenting

1. David L. Goetz, *Death by Suburb: How to Keep the Suburbs from Killing Your Soul* (San Francisco: HarperCollins, 2006), 42.

2. *Boundarying* may not seem like a real word, but it is. It is used mostly in academic disciplines to describe the process of defining and setting boundaries of behavior and freedom.

3. D. P. McNeill, D. A. Morrison, and H. J. M. Nouwen, *Compassion: A Reflection on the Christian Life* (Garden City, NY: Doubleday, 1982), 4.

4. Ibid.

Chapter 8: Parenting through the Seasons: Childhood

1. John Bowlby, *A Secure Base: Parent-Child Attachment and Healthy Human Development* (New York: Basic Books, 1990), 2.

2. Ron Taffel, *Breaking Through to Teens* (New York: Guilford, 2005), 18.

3. As quoted in *Christianity Today online*, C. S. Lewis quote from *Christianity Today* website http://www.christianitytoday.com/tc/2005/006/1.30.html, accessed August 2, 2006.

4. C. S. Lewis, *The Lion, the Witch and the Wardrobe* (New York: Macmillan, 1950), 179–80.

5. This is a quote from a lecture Brennan Manning gave at the Downing House in Denver, Colorado, during an intimate retreat, October 1998.

Chapter 9: Parenting through the Seasons: Early Adolescence

1. The process is primarily concerned with what scholars refer to as "psychosocial development," which is how an adolescent sees themselves in relation to how they perceive others to see and treat them. This is at the heart of the adolescent process.

2. Bowlby, *A Secure Base*, 3.

3. Although there is not enough evidence of this to sway the skeptics of our society, there is ample support to convince scholars who look at the father-child relationship during adolescence.

Chapter 10: Parenting through the Seasons: Midadolescence

1. See chapter 2 for a more detailed description of lengthened adolescence.
2. This is confirmed by the National Study for Youth and Religion in their landmark study of adolescent religion in the U.S. For more information on their findings, see their website at http://www.youthandreligion.org.

Chapter 11: Parenting through the Seasons: Late Adolescence, Emerging Adulthood

1. Carla Barnhill, "The Postmodern Parent: Shifting Paradigms for the Ultimate Act of Re-Creation," in Doug Pagitt and Tony Jones, *An Emergent Manifesto of Hope* (Grand Rapids: Baker, 2007), 41–42.

Chapter 12: Six Longings of Today's Adolescents

1. Quoted at http://www.docsfortots.org (accessed July 14, 2006).

Chapter 13: Parenting as Partnership: The Three Levels of Partnership

1. Henri Nouwen, *Primacy of the Heart* (Madison, WI: St. Benedict Center, 1988), 46.
2. The Hebrew word *ezer* is most often used in military settings and is usually attributed to God as he enters the battlefield to rescue Israel. It is also used to describe God as one who comes in to rescue (hence, "help") someone in need, as in Psalm 79:9: "Help [*ezer*] us, O God our Savior, for the glory of your name; deliver us and forgive our sins for your name's sake."
3. See Malachi 2:14, where God declares, "It is because the LORD is acting as the witness between you and the wife of your youth, because you have broken faith with her, though she is your partner, the wife of your marriage covenant."

Chap Clark (PhD, University of Denver) is the professor of Youth, Family, and Culture at Fuller Theological Seminary, the senior editor of *YouthWorker Journal*, a *Sojourner* "Red Letter Communicator," and president of ParenTeen™ and HURT Seminars. He is a speaker, trainer, consultant, as well as the author of more than sixteen books, including *Hurt: Inside the World of Today's Teenagers* (Baker Academic, 2004, CBA Silver Medalist for Book of the Year) and *Deep Ministry in a Shallow World*. Chap has served in many diverse settings over his career, in the church, parachurch, and industry. He was on the Young Life staff for fifteen years as an area and regional director, and for the past seventeen while a seminary professor, Chap has served as an executive pastor, a senior pastor, and a consulting producer for a New Line television reality show. He is a highly acclaimed resource for community, adult, youth, and family conferences, as well as media, boards, corporate, and educational consulting and training.

Dee Clark is president of Healing Reins, Inc., an author, and a licensed marriage and family therapist in California and Washington. As the founder of Healing Reins, Dee is certified with EGALA, the professional association that trains therapists and counselors for equine-assisted therapy, which uses horses in therapeutic applications. She is a graduate of Colorado Christian University (BS) and Denver Seminary (MA, Counseling) and has done postgraduate work in the School of Psychology at Fuller Theological Seminary in Pasadena, CA. She was also on the Young Life staff for several years. Dee is the coauthor of three books, all with her husband, Chap, including *Let Me Ask You This: Conversations That Draw Couples Together*, and contributed to *Silver and Gold: Stories of Special Friendships*.

Dee and Chap have been married for over twenty-six years, and have partnered together in ministry, as well as speaking and writing throughout their married life. They have three grown children: Chap, Jr. (twenty-six), Rob (twenty-two), and Katie (nineteen). They make their home in Gig Harbor, WA.

You may contact the Clarks at www.ParenTeen.com.

"Teens are frequently hurt psychologically, and they believe that no one really understands them, especially their parents. If you want an understanding of youth culture, of the pressures under which young people live, of the loneliness affecting many teens, and of the angst that your children carry with them, then read this book."

—HENRY HOLSTEGE,
Christian Home & School

"As an advocate for kids for over twenty years, I have watched things change since I was in school. Thankfully, this book made me face what I intuitively knew was real but pretended wasn't: The youth of our culture have been deeply wounded by our collective neglect and adult-driven self-focus. Young people need adults to understand what they are going through and people to care about them without a personal agenda. This book was very helpful to me, and my attitude toward teens will never be the same."

—DOUG FIELDS, pastor to students, Saddleback Church

"This book does a great job of framing the issues affecting adolescents. It provided me with some powerful insights. No wonder adolescents identify with the movies I have been making—the characters are on the same journey of trying to find hope and authenticity. This book is a great look inside the adolescent world, the world beneath the one exposed to adults."

—RALPH WINTER, producer of *Star Trek IV* and *VI*, and *X-Men*

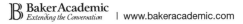

B Baker Academic
Extending the Conversation | www.bakeracademic.com

PARENTEEN SEMINARS

BRIDGING THE GAP BETWEEN TEENS AND THEIR PARENTS

We live in fragmented times—marriages being shattered, families torn apart, and kids having fewer safe and supportive people and places to rely on. We are all scrambling—youth workers, pastors, teachers, coaches, and parents are all trying to figure out how to connect with today's distant and disillusioned teens.

PARENTEEN SEMINARS
For parents of children and adolescents to first understand how the world of their kids is changing and how God is calling them to respond.

HURT: Inside the World of Today's Teenagers Seminar
For youth workers, educators, or for town hall gatherings, this seminar offers both understanding the inside of kids' lives and world and strategies for effectively reaching them.

For more information on arranging a seminar, contact:

Email: info@parenteen.com
Phone: 253-858-9441
www.parenteen.com